Gwendolyn Brooks'
Maud Martha

Gwendolyn Brooks' *Maud Martha:*
A Critical Collection

Edited by

JACQUELINE BRYANT

**With a Foreword
by Nora Brooks Blakely**

THIRD WORLD PRESS
Chicago

Third World Press
Publishers since 1967
Chicago

First Edition
Printed in the United States of America

07 06 05 04 03 02 5 4 3 2 1
Cover design by Denise Borel Billups

Library of Congress Cataloging-in-Publication Data

Bryant, Jacqueline,
    Gwendolyn   Brooks,   *Maud   Martha*:   A   critical
collection/edited by Jacqueline Bryant; with a foreword by
Nora Brooks Blakely. — 1st ed.
    p. cm.
    Includes bibliographical references and index.
    ISBN 0-88378-237-5 (alk. paper)
    1. Brooks, Gwendolyn, 1917 - Maud Martha
    2. African American women in literature.
    3. Middle West — In Literature. I. Bryant, Jacqueline K.

PS3503.R7244 M2833 2002
811'.54—dc21   2002028720

In Memory of Gwendolyn Brooks.
In the Spirit of Kindness.

Contents

Of Mama and Maud
A Foreword

Before you get into the book. Before you can start the story. She says, "Maud Martha was born in 1917. She is still alive." And so she is. There is so much of Mama in Maud . . . and so much of them in me.

I was born in a year that was neatly sandwiched between my mother's Pulitzer Prize and the publication of her novel. As a child I read pieces of *Maud Martha* because it was my Mama's. As an adult, because I should. And after December 3, 2000, I read it as part of my effort to reacquaint myself with this incredible writer. The writer I could now separate (sometimes) from the parent.

Sometimes. Because now, when I read *Maud Martha* the likenesses lurk in every corner. Page after page meets me with memory and mirror. Candy buttons. I confess I still get just a little too happy when I bump into a surprise of paper strips with neat, edible little rows. Sunsets. Our back porch at 74th and Evans, like my mother's other home on 43rd and Champlain, shared its glorious western abstracts every evening. And dandelions. Our backyard not only had a beloved lilac tree but masses of those little chatty, yellow-headed friends. And I, like Mama, Maud, and so many others, have drawn comfort from believing cherishment is not only for the acknowledged Bevies Beautiful.

Not that everything is a copy of the real. Mama had no older sister. Although I suspect that Helen was a stand-in for all of Mama's lighter "sisters." My grandfather, petty-less and patient, bears little resemblance to Maud's father. Just as Maud's "shut-up" woman, who could barely be in the same room with her delivering daughter, does not remind me in any way of my dutiful grandmother, who was sometimes severe

and sometimes a dollop-er of butter and brown sugar on oat-
meal.

But it's not just the story of *Maud Martha* which sparks so
many memories. This collection reminds me of life 'roun'
Mama. I'm reminded (by Bolden) that Maud said, "I wanted
every phrase to be beautiful, and yet to contribute sanely to
the whole, to the whole effect." That is Maud's world but my
mother's words and religion. And I'm constantly reminded of
passages which slap me with the wish that I could write like
that. I remember those four straight, yet disgusted, chairs, the
voices which "sharpened" yet "had fur at the base," and I say
(to Kendrick) yes, "Maud Martha . . . stretches the Ordinary
to the Supreme" . . . and so did her creator. Reflecting on her
regalness (Tsuruta), although Mama would have denied such,
she was determined royalty in her own place and time. Mama
and Maud lived the words ". . . everything can be done with a
little grace. I'm sure of it."

This ground-breaking collection is a major step forward in
the definition and delineation of *Maud Martha*. Historical
information, insights and debate points abound. No, I didn't
know Helen was originally the planned protagonist (Melhem).
And although, it's true my mother's fascination with the "lifeless properties" of gray (Richardson) was woven into her entire
body of work, it was not her only relationship with that color.
She also loved peaceful gray days and rain of soft silver. And
while, "the ramifications of Maud's existence are tied to her
appearance" (Newson-Horst) and, to a lesser extent, impacted
the life and vision of a young, dark-skinned writer, that is not
the whole story. Throughout the changing critique and estimation, Maud was still Maud, and Mama was always Mama,
however the world around them chose to view them.

In her eighties, Mama lived Life and, Moving On, left not
only a legacy of word and wisdom and warmth but shared
much with her two daughters of page and of world: a love of

"foolish food" and fine things, a need for grace, her compass to a fundamental and Center self, and a belief in the sanity and sanctity of tea.

Nora Brooks Blakely

Acknowledgments

I wish to thank Gwendolyn Brooks for being. I thank her for her inspiration and her kindness. I am grateful to have simply been in her presence. Finally, I wish to thank Gwendolyn Brooks for the classic novel, *Maud Martha*, a novel that will challenge readers for centuries to come.

I am grateful to Haki R. Madhubuti for his consistent support and encouragement since our initial discussion of this project in December 1999. Thank you to each member of the staff at Third World Press, especially Ms. Gwendolyn Mitchell. A sincere thank you to each contributor of this collection. Upon receipt of my letter of invitation, contributors responded with enthusiasm and followed through on their commitment. A heart-felt thank you to the late Dr. Maria K. Mootry. My very sincere thanks also goes to contributors Drs. Larry R. Andrews, B. J. Bolden, Kelly Norman Ellis, Regina Jennings, Dorothy Randall Tsuruta, Elaine Richardson, Adele Newson-Horst, D. H. Melhem, and Poet Laureate Dolores Kendrick. A most sincere thanks to Ms. Nora Brooks Blakely. I will always remember her kindness.

A special thank you to Dr. Maria Mootry's mother, Mrs. Helen Rushing, for taking the time to read her daughter's essay and to simply share. I wish to thank Chicago State University community members and English Department Staff members for their ongoing support.

Finally, I wish to thank my husband, Louis Bryant, my daughter, Angela, and my sister, Beverly Johnson, for their ongoing support and encouragement. I also wish to thank my parents, Mr. James C. Peterson and Mrs. Alberta B. Peterson, for their strengthening presence in my life, all my life. For those numerous unnamed supporters of this project, I thank you.

A Chronology

1917	Gwendolyn Elizabeth Brooks is born on June 7th to Keziah Corine Brooks and David Anderson Brooks in Topeka, Kansas. The family moves to Chicago five weeks after her birth.
1930	Publishes her first poem, "Eventide," in American Childhood magazine at the age of 13.
1934	Graduates from Englewood High School in Chicago.
1936	Graduates from Wilson Junior College in Chicago (now Kennedy-King College).
1939	Marries Henry Lowington Blakely.
1940	Gives birth to son, Henry Blakely, Jr., on October 10.
1941	Attends writer's workshop facilitated by Inez Stark.
1943	Wins Midwestern Writer's Conference Poetry Award.
1945	Publishes *A Street in Bronzeville,* her first volume of poetry (Harper & Brothers).
1945	Wins four awards at the Midwestern Writer's Conference.
1945	Becomes one of *Mademoiselle* magazine's "Ten Young Women of the Year."
1945	Receives Society of Midland Authors' "Patron Saints" Award.
1946	Wins first Guggenheim Fellowship.
1946	Becomes a Fellow of the American Academy of Arts and Letters.
1947	Wins second Guggenheim Fellowship.

1949	Publishes *Annie Allen,* her second volume of poetry (Harper & Brothers).
1950	Wins Pulitzer Prize for *Annie Allen;* the first Black to win the Pulitzer Prize for poetry.
1951	Gives birth to daughter, Nora Brooks Blakely, on September 8.
1953	Publishes only novel, *Maud Martha* (Harper & Brothers).
1956	Publishes *Bronzeville Boys and Girls* (Harper & Brothers).
1960	Publishes *The Bean Eaters,* her third volume of poetry (Harper & Brothers).
1962	Reads poetry at a Library of Congress Poetry Festival at the invitation of President John F. Kennedy.
1963	Publishes *Selected Poems* (Harper & Row).
1964	Wins Friends of Literature Award for Poetry.
1964	Wins Thurmon Monsen Award for Literature.
1967	Attends Fisk University Black Writers' Conference.
1968	Publishes *In the Mecca* (Harper & Row).
1968	Becomes Poet Laureate of Illinois.
1969	Publishes *Riot* (Broadside Press).
1971	Publishes *Family Pictures* (Broadside Press); Publishes *The World of Gwendolyn Brooks* (Harper & Row); publishes *Aloneness* (Broadside Press).
1971	Edits *A Broadside Treasury* and *Jump Bad: A New Chicago Anthology* (Broadside Press).
1971	Edits *The Black Position,* a periodical.
1972	Publishes autobiography, *Report from Part One* (Broadside Press).
1974	Publishes children's book, *The Tiger Who Wore White Gloves* (Third World Press).

1975   Publishes *Beckonings* (Broadside Press);
          Publishes *A Capsule Course in Black Poetry
          Writing* with Keorapetse Kgositsile, Haki R.
          Madhubuti, and Dudley Randall (Broadside
          Press).
1980   Publishes *Primer For Blacks* (Black Position
          Press); Publishes *Young Poet's Primer* (Brooks
          Press).
1981   Publishes *To Disembark* (Third World Press).
1983   Publishes *Mayor Harold Washington and
          Chicago, the I will City* (Brooks Press); Publishes
          Very Young Poets (Brooks Press).
1985   Becomes the 29th Consultant in Poetry to the
          Library of Congress.
1987   Publishes *Blacks* (The David Company).
1988   Publishes *Gottschalk and the Grande
          Tarantelle* (The David Company).
1988   Inducted into the National Women's Hall of
          Fame.
1989   Accepts the Senior Fellowship in Literature
          awarded by the National Endowment for the
          Arts.
1991   Publishes *Children Coming Home* (The David
          Company).
1994   Accepts the Medal for Distinguished
          Contribution to American Letters from the
          National Book Foundation.
1994   Accepts the Jefferson Lecturer from the National
          Endowment for the Humanities Lifetime
          Achievement Award.
1996   Publishes *Report From Part Two* (Third World
          Press).
1995   Accepts the National Medal of the Arts.
1997   Accepts the Lincoln Laureate Award.

1997	80th birthday, June 7. Chicago's Mayor Daley announces Gwendolyn Brooks Week in Chicago. Eighty poets and writers attend a special program entitled "Eighty Gifts" in her honor.
1998	Inducted into the International Literary Hall of Fame for Writers of African Descent.
1999	Accepts the First Women Award from First Lady Hillary Clinton during the National First Ladies Library Award ceremony.
2000	Accepts the 65th Academy Fellowship from the Academy of American Poets.
2000	Accepts the Distinguished Achievement Award from the Phi Beta Kappa Honor Society.
2000	Makes her transition, Sunday, December 3.

At a moment like this one could think even of death with a sharp exhilaration, feel that death was a part of life: that life was good and death would be good too.

—Gwendolyn Brooks
Maud Martha

"Home"

Jacqueline Imani Bryant

Ancestor, elder, poet, Queen Mother, mother, grandmother, mother-in-law, sister, daughter, sister-in-law, ambassador, giver, seer, sage, hero, reader, creator, Wordmaker, writer, speaker, artist, novelist, Pulitzer Prize winner, Poet Laureate of Illinois, Distinguished Professor of English, gentlewoman . . . kind.

Born at home on June 7, 1917 to Keziah Corine Wims Brooks and David Anderson Brooks in Topeka, Kansas, Gwendolyn Elizabeth Brooks would become a life-long resident of Chicago, Illinois from her fifth week of life, to her eighty-third year of gracious living, December 3, 2000.

Loving parents and extended family members surrounded the young Gwendolyn Brooks and her younger brother, Raymond Brooks. Possessing the keen observation of a caring mother and a former school teacher, Mrs. Keziah Wims Brooks recognized her daughter's writing talent at the young age of seven years old. Mr. and Mrs. Brooks provided books and created an environment that nourished her talent and her enjoyment of reading and writing. She exhibited the discipline of a seasoned poet when she wrote at least one poem per day and kept notebooks of her poetry at the age of 11 years old. Gwendolyn Brooks became a published poet at the age of 13 years old when *American Childhood* published her poem entitled "Eventide" in October 1930.

The young Miss Brooks continued to read, write, publish, and win numerous awards. During her youth, both James Weldon Johnson and Langston Hughes read her poetry and

1

encouraged her to continue to write. After attending several Chicago area high schools, Gwendolyn Brooks graduated from Englewood High School located on the South Side of Chicago. Following high school, she completed a degree at Wilson Junior College (now Kennedy-King College) in Chicago, and shortly thereafter, married Henry Lowington Blakely in the home of her parents. On October 10, 1940, Gwendolyn Brooks Blakely gave birth at home to her first born, Henry Jr.

One year after the birth of her son, Gwendolyn Brooks attended a poetry workshop led by Inez Cunningham Stark. The workshop leader and Gwendolyn Brooks' fellow work-shop participants contributed to her ongoing growth in the writing of poetry. In 1945, Harper & Brothers published her first book of poetry entitled *A Street in Bronzeville*. The year 1949 marked the publication of Gwendolyn Brooks' second volume of poetry, *Annie Allen*. In 1950, while playing the roles of wife, mother of a 10-year-old son, and published poet, Gwendolyn Brooks transformed historical and literary land-scapes when she won the Pulitzer Prize for Poetry in 1950. She is the first Black to have received the Pulitzer Prize. In 1953, Harper & Brothers publishes Gwendolyn Brooks' one and only novel, *Maud Martha*.[1]

Gwendolyn Brooks writes *Maud Martha,* initially entitled "American Family Brown" (Melhem 80-81), against the back-drop of the political, economic, and social realities of war. As literary artist, Brooks positions the protagonist, Maud, in the home and permits her to filter these significant events in or near the home, through youthful and young adult eyes. The writing, revision, and eventual publication of this seminal work occur within a ten-year period beginning in the early 1940s, during World War II, and ending in 1953, with the Korean War. During the early 1940s, Brooks, like other South Side Chicago residents, experienced, first hand, the housing shortage in the Black neighborhood, food rationing, and the severing of familial ties due to war. The novel clearly reflects these themes. For example, the reader detects Maud's diminishing enthusiasm when she realizes the restrictive and permanent nature of her new home (62). In the chapter entitled "kitchenette folks," the text provides a glimpse of the challenges of residing in a kitchenette dwelling-a dwelling where the most personal aspects of life become the most public acts of living (108). The housing shortage necessitates an ongoing search for better housing. This search results in frequent moves within a politically prescribed area of designated dwellings. In the chapter entitled "back from the wars!", Maud is elated about her brother's safe return from the war in a distant land; however, she struggles with the reality that the war against injustice in the land of America continues (178-179). During the war, food costs increase more than 60% (Trager 876). The chapter entitled "brotherly love" captures the concern about the lack of food and the implication of food rationing when Maud prepares and anticipates a meal that finally includes poultry (153). Thus *Maud Martha* clearly mirrors the context in which it was written, for Brooks delicately weaves aspects of the historical and elements of the literary.

Gwendolyn Brooks contributes to this context of historical and literary events with the publication of her two volumes of poetry, *A Street in Bronzeville* (1945) and *Annie Allen* (1949). Gwendolyn Brooks publishes *Maud Martha* in 1953, a critical period, for James Baldwin publishes his first novel, *Go Tell It on the Mountain,* during the same year. In 1953, Ralph Ellison wins the National Book Award for his first novel, *Invisible Man,* published in 1952. Although Richard Wright has been living in France since 1947, the publication of *The Outsider* in 1953 would still be of interest on the American literary scene (Wright 289). Arguably, the literary accomplishments of Black male writers elicit increased critical response. Black woman writer Ann Petry does, however, enjoy critical acclaim with her novel, *The Street,* seven years earlier in 1946. *Ebony* magazine appropriately entitles an April 1946 article: "First Novel: Ann Petry *defies tradition* and hits the jackpot in *The Street*" (35-39 emphasis mine), for her novel ultimately results in more than 1.5 million in sales. Brooks' having won her first Guggenheim Fellowship in May of 1946, based upon her initial work on "American Family Brown" (*Maud Martha),* surely would be encouraged by the critical reception surrounding Petry's novel. With the renewal of the Guggenheim Fellowship in April 1947, however, Brooks submits "American Family Brown" during that same year only to face rejection (Kent 76; Melhem 82). Undaunted, Gwendolyn Brooks completes and publishes *Annie Allen* in 1949, is awarded the Pulitzer Prize for Poetry for *Annie Allen* in 1950, gives birth to a healthy baby girl in 1951, and, after extensive revisions, publishes *Maud Martha* in 1953. Ann Petry would be among those to render very positive responses to the novel (Kent 112-113). Chicago area reviews are most favorable. Overall, however, the critical reception is mixed.

That Gwendolyn Brooks' *Maud Martha* has fallen short on critical attention during the period of publication and subsequent to that period is a repeated observation. The main purpose of this collection of critical essays is to contribute to the existing dialogue, to increase the volume of the dialogue, and to keep the dialogue ongoing surrounding Gwendolyn Brooks' *Maud Martha.* The critical, scholarly works of the 1980s and 1990s encourage us to continue to engage in the multiple readings that this superb novel invites. It is the hope that Gwendolyn Brooks' *Maud Martha: A Critical Collection* will introduce the novel to some readers, serve as a companion text to the novel for other readers, and lead to the production of similar works.

It is important to note that Gwendolyn Brooks was aware of the work on this collection of essays, for I shared this information with her on May 12, 2000 during an end-of-the-semester, English department dinner. She was most pleased. Of the scholars contributing to this collection of essays on Gwendolyn Brooks' novel, one has made her transition. Maria K. Mootry, a Gwendolyn Brooks' scholar, made her transition on May 29, 2000. Maria Mootry responded immediately to the invitation to contribute to this collection by sending a draft, followed by a final copy of a paper presented at the Society for Study of Midwestern Literature conference during May 1996.

Indeed, each contribution is special, for each reflects a unique approach to this very rich text. Contributor D. H. Melhem graciously consented to submit her published biographical work that provides the historical perspective of the making of the novel, *Maud Martha*. She also summarizes each chapter in the essay entitled *"Maud Martha, Bronzeville Boys and Girls."* Maria K. Mootry illuminates the modernist aesthetic through period-specific art forms in "Gwendolyn Brooks' *Maud Martha: Jivin'* as a Modernist Aesthetic in a Black Midwest Novel." In the essay entitled "Regional and Regal: Chicago's Extraordinary Maud Martha," Dorothy Randall Tsuruta explores the characterization of Maud Martha through temporal and spatial aspects of setting. Larry R. Andrews illuminates the persistence of vitality in the protagonist, despite the ever present, imperceptible, and obvious forces that resist life in "The Aliveness of Things: Nature in *Maud Martha*." In "The Rhetorical Power of Gwendolyn Brooks' *Maud Martha*," B. J. Bolden centers on poetic and rhetorical elements, while Dolores Kendrick captures, the identifiable qualities of Gwendolyn Brooks' *Maud Martha* in her essay entitled "Brooksian Poetic Elegance in *Maud Martha*." Regina Jennings considers Africana Womanism and

5

the social context of racial consciousness in "Understanding Maud Martha through an Africana Womanist Conception: Notions of Self and Gender (Mis)Communication, while Elaine Richardson explores the struggle for social equality in the color motif of gray in her essay entitled "Black is Not Gray: *Maud Martha* as an Argument for Social Equality." In "Selfhood Revealed: Daughterhood, Motherhood and Silences in Maud Martha,"Kelly Norman Ellis foregrounds the multiple meaningful voices of the protagonist, Maud Martha, by illuminating significant aspects of her growth and development. Finally, Adele Newson-Horst explores color consciousness in the character, Maud Martha, through an Africana Womanist lens as she utilizes similar themes in earlier and later works in her essay entitled "Maud Martha Brown: A Study of Emergence."

The voices of these contributors will undoubtedly invite more voices and thus increase the volume of the dialogue, for Gwendolyn Brooks offers in *Maud Martha* not a slice of life, but a full helping-a helping that nourishes the soul, the body, and the spirit. One particular chapter entitled "home" exemplifies this nourishment, for Gwendolyn Brooks creates a landscape that includes the finest details of home and family life. Her language compels the reader to pause, remember, and capture the scene, the intonation, the glance, the gesture. Specifically, Brooks' chapter entitled "home" presents characters teeming with vitality and scenes taut with energy and emotion when Maud's father returns from the Home Owner's Loan office.

Brooks depicts very clearly the extent to which home as sanctuary bears significance for each member of the family. Mrs. Brown and her daughters, Maud and Helen, chatter nervously as they await the results of Mr. Brown's visit. They are so anxious that they attempt to predetermine the outcome by studying Mr. Brown's gait and posture as he moves toward home. The narrator suggests that one should expect posture to reveal "something," but in this instance, it reveals nothing. It is interesting that Brooks' contemporary, Ann Petry, uses this character trait to help define Lutie's father in her 1946 novel, *The Street.* The narrator repeatedly directs the reader's attention to Pop's erect posture as he moves from one battle to another. Whether sober or intoxicated, Pop's posture reflects a Black man in a never-ending struggle-a struggle that surfaces in many forms, even a character trait as inconspicuous as posture. In Brooks' text, however, Mrs. Brown, Helen, and Maud "could not tell a thing from the way Papa was walking. It was that same dear little staccato walk, one shoulder down" (31-32). When Mr. Brown approaches the porch, the text reveals that Mrs. Brown rose "and followed him through the front door" (32). Despite their anxiety resulting from their father's return from the Home Owner's Loan office, Maud and Helen attempt neither to halt their father nor to follow him into the house. Brooks does not depict Maud and Helen demonstrably leaping from their seats, throwing themselves at their father, and pleading that he tell them whether they would have to move from this house that they called home. The gravity of the situation, the controlling presence of the mother, and the respect that both Maud and Helen have for their parents are inextricably linked. Without explanation, elaboration, or justification, however, Brooks simply writes: "The girls knew better than to go in too" (32). It is understood that Mr. and Mrs. Brown are to be alone when Mr. Brown shares the results of his visit to the Home Owner's Loan office. Only his soul mate, Mrs. Brown, could truly understand and appreciate the gravity of the matter, thus Mr. Brown bypasses his daughters with a mere "hello" and communicates volumes in his silence. Mrs. Brown does not demand to know the outcome of his visit in the presence of the girls, but follows her husband into the house. It is in the presence of his wife that

Mr. Brown shares the good news that the family will remain within the confines of this, their very own home.

While Maud clings to memories of her nurturing childhood home, an acquaintance, David McKemster dismisses the memories of his past. McKemster sees home as a place of discomfort and distress and attempts to sever the ties to memories of home and early life experiences. Readers observe evidence of a psychological dislocation resulting from cultural discontinuity when he recalls with disdain that "his mother had taken in washing" (44). McKemster embraces, without question, that which represents the dominant culture. Maud, on the other hand, sees her childhood home as a blue print for the desired home in her adult life. Maud's childhood home was a sanctuary, a place of refuge, and a place of protection. Even though she resides in a kitchenette as an adult, Maud eventually defines and defends her home (167) when she exhibits the strong, silent strength of her father, and yields evidence of cultural continuity and a sense of self. Thus, Gwendolyn Brooks weaves multiple themes of home in the novel, *Maud Martha,* just as the concern for housing permeates the political and economic contexts during the writing of this literary work in the 1940s and publication of the end product in 1953.

Since with the 1990 founding of the Gwendolyn Brooks Center for Black Literature and Creative Writing, Chicago State University has been the national center for the study of Gwendolyn Brooks' life and literary works. Accordingly, her life and works are inextricably woven into the English department curriculum. An excellent example of a course offering is the Gwendolyn Brooks Seminar. The seminar is most exceptional because Gwendolyn Brooks accepted student invitations to visit the class at particular times during the semester. The instructor of record, Dr. B. J. Bolden, often invited English department faculty members to the seminar during the poet's visits. Each time she extended the invitation, I would accept. I am grateful that she extended the invitation for Gwendolyn Brooks' class visit on Monday, October 9, 2000 [2] for this would mark Gwendolyn Brooks' final visit to the Center named in her honor. It was indeed a rich experience and a pleasure to see and hear the students engage the text of Gwendolyn Brooks' novel, *Maud Martha*. How excellent to see Gwendolyn Brooks participate in the critical analysis of her own work. How excellent to hear her praise student analyses and interject autobiographical information in what was a most spirited discussion. While commenting on the chapter entitled "second beau," Gwendolyn Brooks shared that she liked the characterization of David McKemster and offered to read the final paragraph of the chapter:

> He wanted a dog. A good dog. No mongrel,
> An apartment-well-furnished, containing a
> good bookcase, filled with good books in good
> bindings. He wanted a phonograph, and
> records. The symphonies. And Yehudi Menuhin.
> He wanted some good art. These things were
> not extras. They went to make up a good back
> ground. The kind of background those guys had.
> (46)

Her voice and presence transformed a Center into a Sanctuary. The richness of that moment in time and the rightness of that space cannot be replicated. The evening of Monday, October 9, 2000 witnessed the majesty of Gwendolyn Brooks, participating in the Gwendolyn Brooks Seminar, taught by Brooks' scholar B. J. Bolden, held in the Gwendolyn Brooks Center for Black Literature and Creative Writing, two weeks prior to the 10th Annual Gwendolyn Brooks' Writers' Conference. The students responded to the intermingling of the autobiographical and the creative, the aural and the visual, the rhythmic tones, meaningful prose, and sagely pose. Gwendolyn Brooks, exhibiting her usual patience and utter kindness, interacted with the seminar students for nearly three hours, and lingered to speak to them one-on-one following the seminar. The seminar participants will cherish and guard the memory of this meaningful exchange as they continue the study of Gwendolyn Brooks' only novel, *Maud Martha,* for years to come.

In the pages that follow, literary scholars engage in meaningful exchange and critical dialogue that promise to generate more dialogue surrounding the life and works of the great one, the kind one, Gwendolyn Brooks.

Notes

1. See the following texts for early biographical information on Gwendolyn Brooks: Brooks, Gwendolyn. *Report from Part One.* Detroit: Broadside Press, 1972; Kent, George. *A Life of Gwendolyn Brooks.* Lexington: University Press of Kentucky, 1990; and Melhem, D. H. *Gwendolyn Brooks: Poetry and the Heroic Voice.* Lexington: University Press of Kentucky, 1987.

2. Recalling some of Gwendolyn Brooks' life experiences, one observes a pattern of significant events occurring during the autumn of various years. Some of these events are her marriage in September 1939, the birth of her son in October 1940, and the birth of her daughter in September 1951. Gwendolyn Brooks publishes *Maud Martha* in September 1953 and moves into her own home during the autumn of 1953. During early autumn on Moday October 9, 2000, Gwendolyn Brooks makes her final visit to the Gwendolyn Brooks Center for Black Literature and Creative Writing. Sunday, December 3, 2000, Gwendolyn Brooks makes her transition at home.

Works Cited

Brooks, Gwendolyn. *Report from Part One*. Detroit: Broadside Press, 1972.

———. *Maud Martha*. 1953. Chicago: Third World Press, 1993. "First Novel: Ann Petry defies tradition and hits the jackpot in *The Street*." *Ebony* April 1946: 35+

Kent, George. *A Life of Gwendolyn Brooks*. Lexington: University Press of Kentucky, 1990.

Melhem, D. H. *Gwendolyn Brooks: Poetry and the Heroic Voice*. Lexington: University Press of Kentucky, 1987.

Trager, James, ed. *The Peoples Chronology: A Year-by-Year Record of Human Events from Prehistory to the Present*. New York: Henry Holt and Company, 1994.

Petry, Ann. *The Street*. 1946. Boston: Houghton Mifflin Company, 1974.

Smith, Rochelle and Sharon Jones, eds. *The Prentice Hall Anthology of African American Literature*. Upper Saddle River, New Jersey: Prentice Hall, 2000. 1118.

Wright, Richard. 1938. *Uncle Tom's Children*. New York: HarperPerennial, 1991.

One

Maud Martha,
Bronzeville Boys and Girls
D. H. Melhem

American Family Brown, the source of Maud Martha,[1] was conceived as a series of twenty-five poems about an American Negro family (GB/EL, Sept. 28, 1944). In her letter of acceptance for *Bronzeville,* Lawrence had inquired about a prose project and encouraged one as artistically feasible. The poetic conception, never completely abandoned, infuses both the lyric passages and the narrative. The first published section appeared in *Portfolio* (Summer 1945). With minor changes, it is chapter 18 of *Maud Martha,* "we're the only colored people here." Lawrence mildly faulted the use of italics, but admired the universal quality of the work.

Brooks initially submitted *American Family Brown* on January 25, 1945, as a synopsis and ten chapters. These earned her Guggenheim Awards in 1946 and 1947. The poet's covering letter assured that she had eliminated all the italics she could. Having immediately acknowledged the manuscript, the editor wrote back in February, expressing her reactions and those of several readers. Lawrence felt the original plan was hampered by a self-consciousness more suited to poetry than prose. She thought Brooks potentially a first-rate novelist. She commended the author's knowledge of character and her economy and distinctive rhythm in style. But plot, suspense, and dramatic conflict were to be pursued. The editor wondered whether the story was actually a series of

D.H. Melhem. *Gwendolyn Brooks: Poetry and the Heroic Voice.* (c) 1987 by The University Press of Kentucky. Reprinted with the permission of D. H. Melhem and The University Press of Kentucky. Permission granted for use of the original chapter title and pages 80-95. See abbreviation page for abbreviation explanations.

vignettes. One reader liked the lyrical writing but was disappointed by the sociological tone and patent concern with problems of Negro life. The poet would be more successful, the reader felt, if the themes were implicitly expressed through individuals rather than types, plot instead of perspective. Lawrence reminded that Brooks herself wished to present her people as individuals.

Brooks's warm response (Feb. 25) relieved the editor, who replied the next day. The poet did not see her work as near-static vignettes, but something close to that. Although Helen had been the protagonist, her sister, the more emotional Evelina (later Maud Martha), seemed to upstage her in the plot. In the new, proposed synopsis, Brooks would return to her initial focus on Helen, a reversion justified by Evelina's weakness as a character. She accepted elimination of chapter subheads at the editor's suggestion. On March 15, Lawrence wrote back, again with criticisms culled from several readers. Helen, an intellectual and aesthetic figure central to the new plot, became a minor figure and foil to Maud in the published novel. Stuart, Helen's husband, whom the editor now feared would utter the poet's voice more than his own, entirely disappeared.

The following month, Brooks learned of her Guggenheim Fellowship, and in May she journeyed to New York to receive the $1,000 awarded by the American Academy of Arts and Letters. During her stay, she met Lawrence and left with her some new material for the novel. The editor was very pleased with the revision (EL/GB, May 21). She concurred with another reader who saw improvements toward a more relaxed style and diction. The story now began *in medias res*.

Only a few letters were exchanged between May 21, 1946, and January 28, 1947, when the editor wondered whether *American Family Brown* would be completed by the end of the year. The poet was having marital and financial difficulties at the time, as the editor guessed from Brooks's remark that she would have to support herself and her son (Feb. 8). The writer assured, however, that the novel would be ready in May. Her Guggenheim Fellowship was renewed in April; she wrote an excited and happy letter on April 21, announcing completion of the work that morning.

The final consensus on *American Family Brown* ran against it, mainly as being artificial. On October 20, Lawrence wrote a very regretful letter informing Brooks that the manuscript was being returned. The poet replied bravely that she would not be discouraged. Several months later, true to her word, she submitted another manuscript. This time, however, it was poetry, "Hester Allen," which became *Annie Allen*. The prose work was not mentioned again in the correspondence until January 14, 1949, when Brooks turned in her final manuscript of *Annie Allen*. Excited about doing *American Family Brown* from a new point of view, she expected Lawrence to be less than overjoyed at the news. On March 3, in a letter regarding the final manuscript of *Annie Allen*, the editor asked if Brooks were still interested in doing *American Family Brown* as verse. The poet replied that she was, indeed, still interested. In October 1950, Brooks revealed her plans for new works. One was a book of fifty long poems, entitled "Eminent Bronzevillians," deliberately reminiscent of Lytton Strachey's *Eminent Victorians*. Thus the Bronzeville themes persisted, and would continue.

By April 1951 the poet and her son had moved from a temporary stay with her parents to a new apartment at 32 West 70 Street in Chicago, where the family was reunited. She informed Lawrence that her "illness" since her February visit to New York had been confirmed as a symptom of pregnancy. Nora Blakely was born on September 8 of that year. At the time, Brooks was thirty-four-the number of chapters eventually to comprise *Maud Martha*.

The publishing tale of *American Family Brown* was not resumed until January 21, 1952, when a new work of fiction, "Bronzevillians," was sent to Harper's. The poet suggested photographs (and enclosed samples) to be taken by a young Bronzeville photographer, Gerald Cogbill, for inclusion in the volume. Brooks considered the tone warmer than that of *Annie Allen*, and saw it as nearly another book of poems. Lawrence found the manuscript quite absorbing but not yet a finished product (Feb. 26). She was unhappy with the title "Bronzevillians" and was returning both manuscript and pictures.

Brooks submitted The *Maud Martha* Story, her revision of "Bronzevillians," nearly seven months later. Her noteworthy covering letter of September 15 describes her main transition from the *American Family Brown* manuscript. It was Evelina whom she had favored all along. So she decided to build the novel around her, renaming it significantly, she felt, "*Maud Martha*." The new name had clarified the character for Brooks. Lawrence pleasurably anticipated reading the manuscript.

On October 17 the editor wrote a long letter of over three pages giving a detailed criticism of the book. Although the critique represented readings by four editors, Lawrence's own assurance in assessing prose shows clearly. She warmly accepted *Maud Martha* for Harper's with an offer of a $500 advance against royalties. The criticisms were directed toward fuller characterization of *Maud Martha* and keeping the point of view hers. It was proposed that the unpleasant experiences with whites be balanced by a positive encounter to justify the hopefulness she retains. Brooks replied forthwith that the editorial criticisms were helpful and revisions would take about a month. She agreed with Lawrence's reservations about "the literary club," omitted from the final manuscript. The editor submitted the contract for The *Maud Martha* Story on

October 28 with advice not to rush the work and a suggestion on filling in later details about *Maud Martha*'s family.

On December 31, Brooks resubmitted *Maud Martha*; a covering letter explained her revisions. Mainly striving to unify the viewpoint, she had nevertheless kept to the under-stating of detail that supported her impressionism. Lawrence was delighted with the changes (Jan. 23, 1953) but hoped for elaboration on Maud's relationship with her husband. The next month, despite reservations about possible stereotyping of whites, she affirmed that the book would soon be typeset. In a letter dated the same day (Feb. 14), Brooks wrote that she was contemplating buying a house, a longtime dream, the same house in which she lives today.

Lawrence did not expect the novel to be appreciated by a wide audience (March 2). The reviews, however, in Chicago papers (*Tribune, Sun-Times, Daily News*), the *New York Times*, and in California were overwhelmingly good. The literary editor of the *Chicago Daily News,* Van Allen Bradley, and of the *Sun-Times,* Herman Kogan, telephoned her their highest praise. Langston Hughes sent his laudatory *Defender* review. On November 2, Brooks wrote her first letter to Lawrence from her new home, a small, five-room cottage.

The editor visited Brooks in Chicago on March 9, 1954, and the next day wrote her a letter in which "The Life of Lincoln West" is first mentioned. She hoped that the poet's future work would have a universal perspective.

While one may categorize *Maud Martha* as a Bildungsroman, like Jean Toomer's *Cane* it is unique. It covers more time and is more experimental than, say, Betty Smith's *A Tree Grows in Brooklyn*, a book which the poet told me she "intensely enjoyed and admired." Sherwood Anderson's *Winesburg, Ohio,* also much favored, and Hemingway's *In Our Time* are episodic precursors. Together with the latter's *style indirect libre,* both books point to the main approach in *Maud Martha*.

Brooks's vignetting technique has been identified frequently as "impressionistic." Although *Maud Martha* is impressionistic in certain chapters (most notably in the opening "description of *Maud Martha*" and in "spring landscape: detail") that seem to intersperse the work with prose poems, its moral, psychological, and realistic focusing elude this classification. Nor is its emotional surface raw enough to be expressionistic. Features of the narrative combine, moreover, to suggest the distant yet benign presence of Henry James, whom Brooks favors highly.[2] Maud functions as a unifying consciousness, as discussed in James's prefaces, the "fine central intelligence," in R. P. Blackmur's phrase (James, xviii). One remembers, also, the novelist's thesis of giving "a direct impression of life," and his description, in the preface to *The Ambassadors,* of "the process of vision" as seeing "the precious moral of everything" (James, 308), precisely *Maud Martha*'s natural tendency. In fact, her original reading matter in "the young couple at home" was Henry James, but the selection was criticized as improbable (EL/GB, Oct. 17, 1952). *Of Human Bondage,* a good but less subtle choice, misses a fine point of the characterization.

Another significant comparison and contrast may be made with Gertrude Stein's *Three Lives,* particularly the "Melanctha" section dealing with the unhappy young black woman.3 Both Stein and Brooks poetically compress content-Stein, to portray consciousness; Brooks, to express character and feeling. Yet Stein's achievement, despite her compassion, is more stylistic and linguistic than humane. Style tends to blur differences among the simple lives and mentalities of the three protagonists. Melanctha's friend, "the sullen, childish, cowardly, black Rosie" (85), "was careless and was lazy. . . . Rose had the simple, promiscuous unmorality of the black people" (86). "Melanchtha Herbert was a graceful, pale yellow, intelligent, attractive negress. She had not been raised like Rose by white folks but then she had been half made with real white blood" (86). Stein was not singling out blacks (cf. "thrifty german Anna" and Lena's "german patience"). Her stereotyping issued from the social Darwinism then popular. Notwithstanding, such fallacies mar their literary context.

Brooks refers to *Maud Martha* as an autobiographical novel, a fiction based upon and elaborating sundry facts of her life. This is a summary of her random observations (*RPO*, 190-93): "spring landscape: detail" melds impressions of her own schooldays with those of Henry Jr. as she sat in Washington Park, awaiting his dismissal from kindergarten. "[D]eath of Grandmother" refers to the death of an aunt. "[Y]ou're being so good, so kind" depicts the visit of a white schoolmate. She likes "at the Regal" very much. "Tim" tangentially depicts her Uncle Ernest. "[H]ome" describes the Brooks family's struggle with mortgage payments. Although "Helen's" character is a fiction, Emmanuel and Maud (Brooks) are real. "[F]irst beau" and "second beau" are inspired by William (Bill) Couch, not really a beau but the "Adonis" of Brooks's milieu and a member of Inez Stark's poetry workshop (see epigraph to "gay chaps at the bar"). Prominent at the University of the District of Columbia, Couch is editor of *New Black Playwrights*. "*Maud Martha* and New York," eighteen-year-old Maud's recurrent fantasy visit which shows her imagination, artistic tastes, and the penetration of white bourgeois values, makes no mention of Harlem. In "low yellow," Paul primarily recalls "Virgil J_____, who used to live with his grandmother and brother on the second floor of my family home long long long ago, when we were both fifteen." "[A] birth" refers to the impromptu delivery of Henry Jr. in the kitchenette at 623 East 63 Street (cf. Maud, "triumphant" at her successful delivery, and Brooks's own satisfaction). "[A]t the Burns-Coopers'," a "much-juggled" account, builds on the author's brief service as a housemaid. The "tree leaves leaving trees" episode refers to herself and Henry Jr.

Transition from "Evelina" to "*Maud Martha*" involved focusing of character and subtle aesthetic judgments. First, the name "Evelina" is more local-Southern and black in association. It may even recall Fanny Burney's principled heroine in *Evelina, or A Young Lady's Entrance into the World,* and the song "Evelina" in the Harold Arlen and E.Y. Harburg feminist musical comedy adaptation *Bloomer Girl* (1947). More pertinent for Brooks, it evokes "Eveline" in Joyce's *Dubliners,* the home-bound heroine who could not follow her romantic dream. The musicality of "Evelina," however, conveys yielding rather than strength, while the alliteration in "*Maud Martha*" firms the image and broadens the social connotations.

Although Maud grows up accepting her prescribed role as a woman, her name indicates conflicts in disposition and circumstance. "Maud," as noted in the discussion of "Sadie and Maud," derives from the name "Magdalene," the devout converted adulteress in the New Testament. The ambivalence recalls Tennyson's "Maud," grappling with passion and duty. Maud in Brooks's earlier poem is a restricted personality. While *Maud Martha* partly shares this quality, her wholesome libido animates the life which the "thin brown mouse" of the first poem rejects. Martha in the New Testament, the sister of Mary, symbol of Christian faith, was also a doer and a worrier. Collocation of the names "Maud" and "Martha," therefore, suggests the conflict between self-assertion and self-restraint, the desire for freedom and the personal, familial, and social responsibilities-and the economics-that constrain the young woman.

Discrimination, both white and black, by society and by family, conditions *Maud Martha*'s relationship with her husband and braces the narrative framework. Painful incident and withheld approval are the established contours of her environment. Against these negative aspects, however, positive ones reflect Brooks's own experiences during the time of composition. Henry Jr., born in 1940, was a child when the novel was being written; Nora was an infant, born two years before the book was published. The poet's own life-nourishing qualities define her heroine. Angers recede; rage glimmers and gleams; but sanity lights the path. This is not yet the "essential sanity, black and electric," called for in "In the Mecca." Black, certainly, but the current is of low voltage here. Within the context of the early fifties, time of the "silent generation," the Dr. Spock era of the child-centered household, the novel reveals an archetypal, postwar, bourgeois concern with home and family, and aversion to politics.

The opening chapter describes seven-year-old "Maudie," as Brooks thought of her, in her own terms of appetite and affection. We enter immediately a world of sense impressions: taste, color, flowers, the sky, images of Brooks herself who "dreamed a lot" on the top step of her back porch. Sensitive, intelligent, caring, Maud loves dandelions because "it was comforting to find that what was common could also be a flower." Affection is "the dearest wish of the heart of *Maud Martha* Brown." Her older sister, Helen, aged nine, dainty and fair, has love from the entire family, including her brother; Maud makes an early connection between appearance and social value.

"[S]pring landscape: detail," with exquisite pointillism, creates a background of children moving past buildings and "keep off the grass" signs over the seedling grass, children perceived as multicolored bits of clothing carried by "jerky little stems of brown or yellow or brown-black, . . . Past the tiny lives the children blew." Inside and outside the classroom, Maud summons vitality and hope. Yet in emulating the perceived virtues of her parents' marriage, her desire for love results in paradox. Her seeming compensatory moral and intellectual vigor combines with physical disadvantage to alienate her from the family and deny her the very love she needs. Even as a grown woman in "Mother comes to call," she relearns her inability to earn love by being studious and good. By this time, however, she has gained ego-strength, accepting that her parents' values will never correspond with hers.

"[D]eath of Grandmother" fixes an important moment in Maud's consciousness and prefigures her adult confrontation in "*Maud Martha*'s tumor." Comic, grotesque, and noble aspects of the dying woman imprint Maud's hospital visit; she controls her fear of the strange-looking invalid by attempts at conversation. Repelled by the unfamiliar odor of death, Maud recognizes Gramma's new, queenly status, she "who, lying locked in boards with her 'hawhs,' yet towered, triumphed over them." Realities of hospital life, vain cries for the bedpan and attention, the sick who feel for each other, awareness of leave-taking-these fill Maud with compassion and grief, becoming near-introjection of Gramma's own dignity in her hard dying.

In a later chapter, "Tim," Maud's paternal uncle, dies and is viewed in his casket, where he looks like "a gray clay doll." Gray recurs in the novel, and elsewhere in Brooks, as the symbol of death and/or despair (see, for example, "The Last Quatrain" in *The Bean Eaters*). Maud attends to values even more than to her own physical demise. She wonders whether "the world was any better off for his having lived." Incipient skepticism touches her own faith as she turns from God's possible opinion of Tim's life to what Tim might have thought. Aunt Nannie, his widow, powders her face before the funeral because Uncle Tim, oily-nosed himself, had hated a shiny nose in others. The chapter closes with Maud's impressions of the ceremony. She realizes that the hymn, "We Shall Understand It By and By," makes little sense because "by and by" is too late. The sentiment echoes the "Now" of "Appendix to The Anniad" and "Exhaust the little moment" of "The Womanhood."

Racial and interracial themes are deftly handled, the tact ranging from amused insight to irony and controlled rage. In chapter 5, "you're being so good, so kind," a white schoolmate calls. In convoluted acceptance of black and white stereotypes, Maud has carefully opened the windows to dissipate any offensive odor on the premises. She feels she incarnates the whole "colored" race being judged by the entire "Caucasian plan." Fearing and welcoming the visit, she disapproves of her own gratitude which had made the occasion momentous.

The bitter recollection of Emmanuel's offer of a ride in his wagon (in "Helen"), his words to Maud-"I don't mean you, you old black gal"-and Helen's acceptance focus the "black-and-tan" motif. Similarities with Annie of "The Anniad" have been justly pointed out: both Annie and Maud are rejected by their lovers because of socially valued lightness and appearance in general.[4] Additionally, Annie functions within the larger context of war's psychic erosions and the fallacy of misplaced romanticism. Maud experiences some disillusion but maintains the optimism of a relatively comic view of life, as opposed to Annie's somewhat tragic one.

"[L]ow yellow" defines Maud's abject satisfaction that her "low-toned yellow" fiancè has chosen her dark, unattractive self because she is "sweet" and "good," Maud still trying to earn love. Their marriage soon founders upon intellectual and sexual differences. Maud submerges her cultural interests in bourgeois aspirations. Like the young *Annie Allen*, she romanticizes Paul's shortcomings, translates his frugality into a pioneer virtue she can admire in them both. Seeking a moral and secular faith, she imagines herself "dying for her man." Much later, she sees him as crude and superficial. "Clowning" to get her attention as they return from a musicale (remember the dignified Negroes who "would not clown" in "I love those little booths at Benvenuti's"), refusing to borrow a book from the library, looking only to see whether there was an author named "Bastard" in the author index (which there was), waiting until Christmas morning to buy a tree inexpensively, exchanging Maud's richness of family life and its holiday memories for one in which she struggles to establish traditions. Especially after the birth of her daughter Paulette, Paul becomes a man who "could eat from a splintery board, he could eat from the earth."

Segregation makes for a painfully self-conscious visit to the movie in "we're the only colored people here." But the black-and-tan dilemma more cruelly afflicts Maud at the Annual Dawn Ball of the Foxy Cats Club, a group of pleasure-seekers. Pregnant, watching Paul dance with the redhead, she realizes that her color will always be "like a wall. He has to jump over it in order to meet and touch what I've got for him. . . . He gets awful tired of all that jumping." After the birth of Paulette, at which Mrs. Brown plays impromptu midwife, Maud jubilantly advances toward maturity. Reference to the new grandmother as "Belva" instead of "Mama" equalizes mother and daughter. Maud's full married name appears for the first time: "Maud Martha Brown Phillips." The child's beauty is a welcome surprise. Later, drinking wine with "Paul in the 011 Club," Maud thinks, "The baby was getting darker all the time!" as if listing another failure Paul might escape by joining the military service. This is the first citing of the war, and the issue remains personal.

Maud's ambivalence, her inward struggles between realism and romanticism, passivity and rebellion, domesticity and culture, determine the narrative sequence. The pattern, usually alternating between lyrical and descriptive modes, maintains the pace and tension from one vignette to the next. For example, "first beau," symbolically unnamed, awakens Maud's sexual desires (no longer dream-disguised, as in the Freudian "love and gorillas"). His lyrical portrait echoes the young *Annie Allen*'s gallant paladin ideal, one who has ways with "a Woman." This episode follows the "Helen" chapter's psychological realism contrasting the sisters, with Helen sensually fluffing on "Golden Peacock" powder (gold, the recurrent, illusive symbol in Brooks, acquires from "Peacock" connotations of arrogance and pride) and assuring Maud, "You'll never get a boy friend . . . if you don't stop reading those books." And following the impressionistic "first beau," "second beau" realistically presents Maud's romanticized identification with David McKempster [McKemster] and his intellectual yearnings. The two beaux illustrate Maud's conflicting wishes at eighteen for domesticity, affection, and the intellectual good life.

Both Maud and David are misfits; he reappears as a parvenu in "an encounter," years after Maud has entered motherhood. In their chance meeting, he disillusions the young woman by his white-imbued academic and social pretensions; she has already discarded her illusions about marriage. Brooks's symbolic eloquence of detail sparks the Jungly Hovel campus scene. Maud (who has attended a lecture at the college), David, and his two white friends (an engaged couple whose company he prefers to Maud's), await their order. In the ironic closing sentence, a waitress brings "coffee, four lumps of sugar wrapped in pink paper, hot mince pie." Pink, in context, suggests affectation and David's white orientation. "Hot mince pie" is another white cultural touch. Its chopped and mixed ingredients, their individuality further surrendered in baking, connote David's assimilationism.

Contemplative "posts" follows the traumas of "a birth." The quietly lyrical passage sets forth the virtues of a plain marriage, an order of constancy in nature underlying a "system of

consciousness of marriage

change." Maud supposes that the search for a secure relationship may be essential. "Leaning was a work," she concludes. But the truce represents also a defeat for the independent self. "[T]radition and *Maud Martha*," however, succeeds "posts" and Maud's congestive dissatisfactions.

By antithesis and comparison, Brooks defines character and growth. "[K]itchenette folks," whose modest circumstances precede "encounter," inscribes Maud's social eclecticism and breadth of interest. It presents alternate views of marriage. The lively account memorably sketches neighbors such as the doorkey child Clement Lewy, who bravely takes care of himself while his mother, "gray"-looking, deserted by his father, works as a housemaid (anticipating Maud's employment in "at the Burns-Coopers'"); and the "Woman of Breeding," reclusive Miss Snow, who serves herself afternoon tea. Mostly hard-working and appealing, the neighbors reflect Maud herself.

Augmenting the tensions of the "encounter," "the self-solace" beauty salon episode permits Maud's cumulative angers to surface. The white cosmetics saleswoman, who comments unthinkingly that she "works like a nigger to make a few pennies," activates Maud's political consciousness, prefigured at seventeen in "Helen." There the "untamableness" of her hair (cf. "Taming all that anger down" in "The Anniad") offends her father's sense of order and sets her apart even more.

"[M]illinery," in which Maud refuses to buy the suddenly discount-priced hat, is reinforced by "at the Burns-Coopers'," where the heroine, responding staunchly to financial difficulties, accepts a position as maid. The employer's stringent demands echo in her mother-in-law, an imperious woman "with hair of a mighty white." Maud gains insight into the daily indignities Paul suffers on his job. He, too, has an officious "Boss" who views him stereotypically as a child. In a positive act of refusal, confirming that of "millinery," Maud decides not to return. She asserts her humanity: "one was a human being." She has progressed from acceptance of color stratifications-in family, school, marriage, and society-to rebellion.

Maud loves her father, whose imperfect acceptance repeats itself in her relationship with Paul. In "love and gorillas," she rejoices at Papa's return after his argument with her mother; in "home," when he arrives with a crucial mortgage loan, the welcome points up Maud's affection and their basic family solidarity. Papa's "dear little staccato walk" seems as evocative as the hands of Theodore Roethke's father in "My Papa's Waltz," or the mother's "small, poised feet" on the piano pedals as recollected by D. H. Lawrence in "Piano." In "Helen," a touching passage describes the homely, beloved house, cherished so deeply by Maud and her father; its kitchen chairs that "cried when people sat in them," inviting parallel with Maud herself: she who is not beautiful but serviceable, like the house, and who, like the chairs, also cried, alone in the pantry, when feeling abused.

Maud's relationship with her mother remains unresolved. In "a birth," annoyance at Mrs. Brown's obtrusive concern with appreciation gives way to the thought that it might be "as hard to watch suffering as to bear it." Still, Maud must retain the old hurt. In "Mother comes to call," despite wartime austerity, she entertains her visitor with the elegance available for "Tea," the ceremony recalling the "Woman of Breeding" in "kitchenette folks." Dignity and decorum preside over the relationship (witness the formality of "call" in the chapter title). It is Mama who brings tidings of Helen's forthcoming, security-inspired marriage to the family doctor. Mama's pride in the match and disapproval of Paul (she brings food gifts, of which only one pecan is for him) contrast with Maud's disapproval of the union. And when Maud wistfully observes how siblings can differ in appearance and charm, Mrs. Brown, missing the cue, assures her that she is "wonderful" and makes "the best cocoa in the family." Though subdued, the conflict suggests the daughter's continuing development.

In the penultimate chapter, "tree leaves leaving trees," the chiasmus of the title conveys joining and continuity, which persist in tension with losses, change, and growth, themes of the painful visit to Santa Claus. Anticipation fills the child-like listing in the introductory paragraph (with only two commas in the verbless sentence) of twenty-nine different toys for sale in the department store. In a stunning rejection of her blackness, Santa ignores Paulette. Maud's rage distinguishes her from Helen, who would have dismissed the matter, and Paul, who would have been angry momentarily. With this insight, Maud steps importantly toward self-identity, even though "those scraps of baffled hate" remain.

Maud insists to Paulette that Santa really loves her; she wants her daughter to share the beauty of her own childhood faith. The mother's silent cry "Keep her that land of blue!" recalls Langston Hughes's injunction "Hold fast to dreams."[5] Her plea is for the Romantic imagination and for the sustaining early sense of a world where love overcomes evil. Her idealism rejects her own mother's materialism.

Maud's ability to give love; her maturing perception of herself in relation to others (parents, husband, child); her merging of affectionate, intellectual, and artistic impulses within an increasingly vital, moral synthesis: these become beauties of the novel. In "at the Regal," Maud aestheticizes her morality with one "bit of art": "What she wanted was to donate to the world a good Maud Martha." Coming to terms with a sense of alienation and diminished worth, she evolves her personal meaning of "goodness." In the black singer's performance, she perceives discontinuity between art and life. Her gradual countering with existential values mildly rebukes aestheti-

part of Maud's growth involves an acceptance of reality & this color consciousness?

cism.[6] Reverence for life in "Maud Martha spares the mouse," restated pragmatically by "brotherly love," where Maud eviscerates a chicken, defines her achievement. Sparing the mouse, Maud discovers, "I am good," and reaffirms both precedence of life over art and life *as* art. "In the center of that simple restraint was-creation."

"[B]rotherly love" expresses the parallel antiwar theme. Nostalgia for "the happy, happy days" of her childhood mounts against her grotesque, butcher-knife struggle with the anonymous chicken, then combines into meditation on killing in war. Chickens, Brooks's recurrent image of the sacrificial victim (cf. "Sunday chicken," *Annie Allen*), will be safe in the world when people become familiar with them as individual creatures possessed of dignity. We infer an analogy with black-white relations. "What was unreal to you, you could deal with violently" also anticipates the lynching reference in the final chapter.

For Maud, life becomes humanistic faith and its joy. Reprieved from her contemplation of death in "Maud Martha's tumor," her equanimity comprises strength and a measure of weariness with a life she first judges as not "bad" and then "interesting." Yet her resilience as she rushes home bespeaks the author's own adaptive stamina.

In the last chapter, "back from the wars!" (again lyrical, following the Santa Claus incident), Maud's brother Harry has safely returned. Aware of her youthful vigor and hopes, she raises the shade to let in the morning light of reality. "What, *what* am I to do with all of this life?" she muses, expressing the essence of youth, its seeming endlessness. Racial troubles persist. Although the Negro press largely mirrors the white, carrying on its front pages lovely, pale, elegant women, inside, like the recessed anger in Maud herself, there are stories of Southern lynchings. Contemplating nature, however, reveals her own truth: "the basic equanimity of the least and commonest flower" would return in the spring. This Wordsworthian "natural piety" reverts to chapter 1. As the weather bids her "bon voyage," in the first passage written for the novel, Maud embarks upon another journey, expecting a second child.

Maud Martha abides for Brooks, who has planned a sequel-again largely autobiographical. In one version (Hull) the heroine will have three children, become widowed, fall in love at fifty or thereafter, and visit Africa-and all the while her feminist awareness deepens.

This little-appreciated masterpiece of classic simplicity and poetic precision, through an epiphanic mode, weaves dream and reality, philosophy and episode, individual psychology and social milieu. *Maud Martha* has a special significance in Brooks's development of breadth: the ability to project various characters and moods, to sustain a narrative, to balance the sequential with the episodic-all of which look ahead to her major work, *In the Mecca*. Themes of black-and-tan and black-and-white, of love and death, present from *Bronzeville* onward, lattice the personal narrative within the social frame. Her heroine's dilemma typifies the pre-women's liberation either-or choice between domestic duties and self-fulfillment, where attempts at flight were contained within the flock. Maud has learned to adapt, while maintaining the ego-strength that permits change and preserves dreams. One suspects from the novel that her passivity will continue to lift. Although her rationalizing sometimes works against her, it also bolsters her life-assertiveness. A frayed but tenacious idealism and anger spark Maud's consciousness and activist potential.

Like her heroine, Brooks moves on affirmatively to the statements of *The Bean Eaters* and toward prophetic and heroic utterance. What we hear in *Maud Martha*, nevertheless, is the sense of dignity which makes that latent voice elsewhere audible.

Abbreviations

The following abbreviations are used throughout the text
and in the notes:

BSM   Dudley Randall. Broadside Memories:
           Poets I Have Known. Detroit: Broadside Press.
           1975.

BWW   Claudia Tate, ed. *Black Women Writers at Work.*
           New York: Continuum, 1983.

EL   Elizabeth Lawrence

GB   Gwendolyn Brooks

GMR   Langston Hughes. *Good Morning Revolution.* Ed.
           Faith Berry. Westport, Conn.: Hill, 1973.

RPO   Gwendolyn Brooks. *Report from Part One.*
           Detroit: Broadside Press, 1972.

WGB   Gwendolyn Brooks. *The World of Gwendolyn
           Brooks.* New York: Harper and Row, 1971.

References

1. Gwendolyn Brooks, *Maud Martha* (1953), rpt. In WGB, 125–306.

2. Henry James, *The Art of the Novel: Critical Prefaces,* introd. R. P. Blackmur (New York: Scribner's, 1934).

3. Gertrude Stein, *Three Lives* (1909; rpt. New York: Random House/Vintage, 1958).

4. Annette Oliver Shands, "Gwendolyn Brooks as Novelist," *Black World 22* (June 1973): 22–30.

5. Langston Hughes, "Dreams," in *The Dream Keeper and Other Poems* (New York: Knopf, 1932), 7.

6. See Stephen Crane, Maggie: *A Girl of the Streets* (1893). The impressionistic descriptions of theatrical performances that Crane ironically calls in the novel "transcendental realism," uniting Maggie, the audience, and the performers, are recalled in this chapter.

after lengthy preparation of a cultured "snack," rye crackers, pimento cheese and homemade cocoa, Paul consents. After partaking, however, he tires and falls asleep, his book slipping to the floor. Meanwhile, Maud is left with her text, significantly, Somerset Maugham's *Of Human Bondage,* a tale of a mismatched couple (the man educated and upwardly mobile, the woman uneducated and lower class), and their increasing alienation.

On the bus ride home, Paul 'jives' Maud physically, kidding her with what she considers childish physical jokes-little "tricks," cocking his head sideways at her, winking at her, poking her slyly in the ribs, perhaps a reference to Eve's having been made from Adam's rib (?), lifting her hand to his lips, blowing on her hand softly, poking a finger under her chin, raising her chin awkwardly, feeling her muscle, then putting her hand on his muscle, so that she could tell the difference (65-66). This jive love-play in front of total strangers annoys Maud Martha, but she feels gently trapped, "and because he felt that he was making her happy, she tried not to see the uncareful stares and smirks of the other passengers-uncareful and insultingly consolatory"(66). At this point, Paul, the male, has the upper hand with his playful "mating rituals."

Maud is uptight; she wants dignity. Paul, in public view, tries to "soften" her up, make her relax by his kidding and his "jive" so that he can have a pleasant end to his night out. A night he has "endured" for *her* sake. Maud wants more than jive; he even playfully kicks her toe for heaven's sake. She thinks disappointingly to herself: "He could make a comment or two on what went on at the musicale, or some little joke . . . . everything can be done with a little grace. I'm sure of it" (66). The joke here is that Maud is being a bit selfish, and naïve. "Everything can be done with a little grace." The narrator conveys these thoughts with a "straight face," but we get the sly yet gentle satire. Maud has bought into a bourgeois ideal of woman as repository of manners and culture. With her assimilation aspirations, (she attends a "musicale" remember), she looks down on earnest, awkward Paul.

A bit pretentious, then, Maud wants to rise above certain *jivin'* aspects of her folk culture, yet, as we see with her distracting Paul from sex to food, she is not above "jivin'" to get what she wants, just as Eve "jived" Adam, tempting him with the apple. Maud, like ambitious Eve wants "knowledge," but it is knowledge as cultural status. If she can't get this kind of intellectual companionship, then like Greta Garbo, she simply wants to be "left alone."

The narrative voice achieves a "two-step pattern" in this compressed episode. It describes, but the description is "thickened" with double entendre-a form for jivin' the reader. By nuance we are told of Maud's selfish pretensions. A closer look at Maugham's long, wordy novel by a second-tier English writer (not "great" literature) yields a co-narrative that enriches Brooks' terse text. But, is Maud really in a state of "human bondage," or is this her exaggerated response to the banality of married life? Finally, with authorial winks, we are told glibly: "*Sex in the Married life* is about to slip to the floor. She did not stretch out her hand to save it" (68).

"an encounter"

In "an encounter," jivin' is seen in situational irony and in literary allusions. Jivin' on a micro-level expends to a macro-critique that anticipates multicultural revisionism of Western canons. The chapter recounts in brief a chance encounter between Maud and a friend, who "bump" into each other at The University of Chicago after attending a lecture by "the newest young Negro author." This appellation itself suggests a narrative wink as if to assure us that Black writers do not come by twos or threes but only by the latest ONE sensation. I suspect Brooks has in mind James Baldwin. Maud correctly guesses that upon waving to her friend, she will find him cold, and make her feel that she does not belong in his Hyde Park, intellectual, elite integrated setting. She is right. He hardly speaks as he reluctantly acknowledges her wave, and is rushing to get rid of her by jively suggesting that he "see her" to the streetcar, yawning "God, I'm tired" (128). Oh, the games people play! All this "jive" disappears when David runs into a white University of Chicago couple. His face lights up and suddenly he is bright-eyed and busy tailed. He and the couple begin to talk of mutual acquaintances and events; a jive way of shutting Maud out and "bonding" with them. Before he remembers his "burden," David suggests that they visit a friend, Powers, who he jokes, will no doubt be sprawled out on a white rug, reading Parrington. Parrington constitutes the idea of the sociology of knowledge as "jive," i.e. as establishing status credentials. Earlier in the chapter entitled "second beau," David worries about how he has not yet "mastered" Parrington's *Main Currents in American Thought* . . . (43). He feels manqué because unlike those younger than he, David McKemster has not heard it discussed at the dinner table (he is from the ghetto), has not seen it kicked around for years like football (43-44).

Now David, anticipating a night with friends discussing Parrington, searches for another jive trick to get rid of Maud. He suggests buying her coffee at a local eatery. Here the narrator tweaks our sense of fun, by jivin' the characters. David suggests the Jungly Hovel (probably a play on the Tropical Hut, a local Hyde Park restaurant), a name that punctures David's pretensions and makes his situation ironic. He never guesses how disjunctive it is for him, an African-American with intellectual pretensions, to propose dining in a fake trop- ical setting, a kitsch recreation of his "motherland" which he would no doubt scream if anyone suggested that Africa con- stituted his "roots." Jungly Hovel as a title functions oxy- moronically, another "two step" in the narrative.

The white couple, "Stickie" and "O'Brien," like two people

on safari, stare at Maud, this unusual phenomenon in elite Hyde Park. The narrator sarcastically internalizes the man's thoughts: *"Well! . . . Well! What have we here!"* (emphasis mine 130). Maud and David become the objects of "entertainment," a "jive," for Twinkie and O'Brien. The woman, faking sincerity, assumes straightforward body language, but she is jiving: "She was confidential, she communicated everything except herself, which was precisely the thing, her eyes, her words, her nods assured you she *was* communicating" (130-131). Suddenly the narrative jerks, twirls, and takes a turn as David, significantly looking *down* on Maud, begins to discuss the lecturer. David is perturbed. The lecturer had been amazing, had read, well . . . he couldn't supply the word . . . in a moment of syncopation, and Maud with a call-and-response jazz-like hidden echo, chirps in the fatal words: "Everything" (131). Thus is David reduced to improvising, to toying with his two disturbing encounters. The more serious encounter is not between David-Maud, but among all University of Chicago types and the rebel intellectual who revise their pretensions. The new black lecturer, having read Kafka and current intellectuals, in Ellison's words, "changes the joke and slips the yoke." Resisting the current academic sociology of knowledge, he scuttles the classics-the stalwart of University of Chicago elitism, including Aristotle, Plato, and Aeschylus-not to mention the three-volumed Parrington. He rides the top of the new wave, leaving behind David and his colleagues and their jive use of words like anachronism, metaphysical, corollary, . . . (132).

Even as David implies he is secure in his thoughts, he realizes what a trick the lecturer has played. The lecturer has punctured "faith" "in all those [-]damn Greeks" (133). David thinks bitter thoughts and finally loses his ability to verbally jive with wit and brilliance, resorting to the banal observation that "Aristotle is probably Greek" (133) to the rising new author/star. This observation brings a tired but polite response from David's friends. The couple he has striven to impress are no longer "jived." The woman gives a brief laugh. The man smiles but resorts to a more basic reflex; he simply leers at Maud.

David's ploy for acceptance is up when he tells that the lecturer is not in school, and that the lecturer had savagely asked: "What are degrees . . ."? (132). David has been jivin' himself, his white friends and Maud, and now he has met a master jiver. We are in on the joke when he thinks self-centeredly and bitterly: "So he was brilliant. So he could out chatter me. So intellectuality was his oyster. So he has kicked-not Parrington-but Joyce, maybe around like a football" (132-133).

"The encounter" ends when a waitress arrives and plunks plain fare on the table: "coffee, four lumps of sugar wrapped in pink paper, hot mince pie" (133). Though the economical list of food items, the narrator ends both the lesser and the more serious forms of jiving, kidding, dishonesty, deception, nonsense, glibness, and misleading phoniness.

Below the stratum of our cultural pretensions and social games people play, we are simple beings, who, like the people in Brooks' poem on Chicago's Picasso, burp and like to have a beer handy. Jivin' as literary technique lends deeper structure and convoluted meaning to Brooks' text. It suggests a modernist form of indeterminacy as well as the deconstruction of traditional moral, aesthetic, and cultural values. It flirts with nihilism: In the silence of married life going stale, and of friendship floundering on pretentious grounds, we come close to feeling that life has little nobility or high morality. But these satiric chapters must be balanced with other moments in the text. For Brooks, life is full of jive, but not all of life is simply all that jive.

Note

Dr. Maria K. Mootry presented this paper on May 24, 1996
at the Society for Study of Midwestern Literature, East
Lansing, Michigan, May 23–25, 1996.

Three

Regional and Regal:
Chicago's *Extraordinary* Maud Martha

Dorothy Randall Tsuruta

> *that every grace divine/*
> *should with full luster in . . .*
> *conduct shine*
>
> —Phillis Wheatley
> "On the Death of the Rev. Mr. George Whitefield"

The regal and the regional characterize Maud Martha. Although orchestrated into life as the dutiful daughter of loving parents, and later the resolute wife and especially doting mother, Maud Martha also helps herself to her own wonderfully sustaining healthy morale. Her regal bearing can thus be appreciated in her poetical connection to her own humanity as well as that of others. The narrator speaks of her as having "noble understanding"(35) under pressure. And Maud Martha herself confides, "everything can be done with a little grace. I'm sure of it"(66). Her regal bearing is inherent in her outlook on life, in her poise, both intellectual and physical, and in her comportment as she straddles the contradictions in life. Of Maud Martha's literary creator, Gwendolyn Brooks, observes Haki R. Madhubuti (then Don L. Lee): "Her movement into poetry is a profound comment on her self-confidence and speaks to the poetic vision she possessed" (*Report from Part One 15*). This poetic vision is at the heart of the nature of this woman who, in recreating in novel form the *human elegance* of Maud Martha, brings attention to a feature too often ignored in printed and spoken discussions that single out the Black woman's strength of back and character (one thinks of Sojourner Truth) at the expense of her *extraordinarily* earned expectation of chivalrous respect for her humanity.

Brooks' *Maud Martha* is a Chicago story in that this place, in the manner of regional identities, has its own personality formed by the preponderance of contributions to its identity. For just as in music there is a Chicago sound in jazz, so too there is a Chicago sound in the human groove—albeit this is easier to say than to prove by way of a fail-safe prototype. Maria Mootry avows that "for Brooks, region ultimately meant not only the Midwest and metropolitan Chicago but also, more specifically, southside Chicago"(6), and I concur with her. My contention that this is a Chicago story, however, rests not only on the geographical evidence, as in the mention of streets (Forty-Seventh and South Park), a theater (Regal), clubs (Club 99 and 011), and other attractions, but on the contention that in that place a particular personality emerges—a particular verve with a definite kind of nerve.

A regal Maud Martha grows up in Chicago from childhood to adulthood so self aware from her earliest meditation, at the outset of the novel, of what she likes about herself, that problems posed by others' shortcomings, become obstacles to which she brings strength of mind and character to bear in "warding off attacks upon her dignity, and maintaining her integrity" (Kent, *A Life of Gwendolyn Brooks* 114-115). Maud Martha's own extraordinary sense of self underscores a quality in southside women that self-informs them of their finer aspects. It is not "strained optimism" (Kent 116) that makes her happy, but real genuine human conceit of a healthy order. Some onlookers appear to find it an impossible feat to believe that with all the public bashing of the dark skinned and Negroid sculpted black woman, she could be quite taken with her own loveliness. And yet Black women saddle that contradiction as they contend with both publicized images of beauty which ravish the public's outlook, and internal enjoyment and acceptance of self. Her many hair and skin products, notwithstanding, the Black woman does not turn pathologically to others for self-approval as Shaw suggests when he writes about Maud Martha: "Although she thinks the dandelion is pretty, she is aware that others consider it plain or ugly —a weed (*A Life Distilled* 257). Being aware of what others think means having the sense to be ever alert to one's environment and world; however, Black women's awareness of how others view them does not necessarily indicate a causal relationship with succumbing to those views, for as June Jordan poetically asserts in "Who Look At Me": "black face, black body and black mind/beyond obliterating" (*Naming Our Destiny* 8).

The heroine of this novel has a quick sardonic wit that discerns and checks the arrogance of those upon whom she comes. That very humor in Maud Martha's veins is also what helps keep her at a safe distance from others' contagious and maddening absurdities that do not elude her. More to the truth is a self-appreciative reading of the novel, in which what others make of the dandelion is a moot point, considering Maud Martha's invincible personal authority. In pursuing this concern, my objective is to show that in the opening chapter Maud Martha is putting the spotlight on what she likes about a dandelion. Thus, a fully respecting self along with a challenging, yet affirming, region contribute to Maud Martha's "racial consciousness with its attendant pride, pain, and defiance" (Mootry 6).

Of course it is easy to walk into a self-set trap trying to define what marks a work as regional, for the very same elements of that work are to be found in another region. In fact what makes *Maud Martha* mightily embraced by many Black people, worldwide, who read it, is the familiar nature of the story. It is either about you, if a Black female—or if you are a Black male, you also find it familiar beyond bringing to mind the Black women in your family or acquaintance. Additionally, *Maud Martha* is familiar across human divides for as Barbara Christian keenly observes, in *Maud Martha* "there are universal moments in that human beings, whatever their race, sex, or class, muse about the meaning of existence and the degree of responsibility they must take to shape their lives" (*Black Feminist Criticism* 133).

Maud Martha is also a Black Diaspora story in that the heroine is removed by Middle Passage from the motherland, and distinguished by race from the majority group in power that has a history of abuse of that power. Yet, Diaspora Black women and men have only to find themselves among fellow Blacks on the African continent to comprehend that what's familiar about *Maud Martha* is similarly what's familiar about their Black kindred in the motherland.   In like manner, African women and men who travel from Africa to places throughout the African Diaspora may just be as apt to marvel at what they find familiar about their scattered kindred who are the descendants of enslaved Africans, forced from home against *will* centuries ago. Maud Martha is familiar because she has the persistence of the Market Woman in regions throughout Africa—just as in her hometown, Chicago, "Maud emerges as a persistent and very tough contender" (Kent 115).

Maud Martha is persistent even when she and her husband decide to go to a theater north of the southside where it's clear that "we're the only colored people here." Her self-consciousness of the fact is not due to any inferiority complex on her part, but rather that on the part of well heeled white onlookers whose benign ostracism is hardly anyone's idea of fun company when splurging on an evening out on the town. But the couple have fun anyway, for as George E. Kent proclaims, "Whatever dignity and beauty arise from [Brooks'] people must . . . be seized from the quality of their struggles and in their assertion of options despite imposing oppositions" (*A Life Distilled* 31). Adding to this aspect of the present discussion, is Houston A. Baker Jr.'s view that "Brooks has often excelled the surrounding white framework and she has been able to see clearly beyond it to the strengths and beauties of her own" (*A Life Distilled* 28). Brooks' ability attests to a certain verve and nerve inherent in those Black women we so admire (despite contrary attempts of caricature on afternoon talk shows and most notoriously whenever the Wayon brothers see fit to abuse humor with distasteful mockery of Black women).

Transcending the physical limitations of a single individual, Maud Martha calls attention to Black girls and women of a particular verve who have the nerve to self-appreciate, self-validate, self-rescue, self-determine, and self-direct. In *Report from Part One,* Brooks tells Ida Lewis about her mother's nerve: "I met [James Weldon] Johnson in person . . . thanks to my mother. She had all kinds of "nerve . . . [she] told me to go up to him"(173). Black mothers, other female relatives, church members, dedicated school teachers, along with others who take an interest in growing girls of their likeness, pass on to their impressionable charges the nerve to expect to be appreciated. This self-acclaiming quality which I argue is one of the defining traits that figure in the composite southside Chicagoan, is noticed by Barbara Christian who speaks of Maud Martha as "not just a creation of her external world; she helps to create her own world by transforming externals . . ." (*Black Feminist Criticism* 132) according to what she has enough sense to understand and act on. Christian goes on to declare: "This is a quality seldom attributed to [Black people] in previous black women's novels" (132). The nerve, here, stamps it a Chicago story, notwithstanding the fact that it is a nerve familiar throughout Africa and other African Diaspora women.

The ability to flirt with western and other non-African poetics (i.e. sonnets through Haiku), yet remain utterly in love

and faithful to African aesthetics, is yet another aspect of
Gwendolyn Brooks, the Chicago author. In comparing the
European novel to the African novel, Emmanuel Obiechina
brings attention also to what's African about *Maud Martha*.

> [T]he sort of formal distance which Walter
> Benjamin assumes when he says 'What
> differentiates the novel from other forms of
> prose literature . . . is that it neither comes
> from oral tradition nor goes into it' . . . would
> be of little validity when applied to the African
> novel. In Benjamin's view, 'The storyteller takes
> what he tells from experience, his own or that
> reported by others . . . the novelist has isolated
> himself.' In the African novel, the embedding
> of the story produces a totally different
> narrative and epistemological situation. The
> African novel is not a sole product of an
> individual consciousness (even though the
> novelist is a conscious individual artist), but is
> mediated by communal consciousness and
> impulses arising from group sensibility. (125)

As notes the recently deceased Barbara Christian who
brought sagacious observation to Black life, "In illuminating
Maud Martha's specific individuality, Brooks . . . show[s] her
in relation to other people and her physical environment"
(*Black Feminist Criticism* 132). Brooks' interview with George
Stavros provides a point of reference here. As the interviewer
queries her about the appropriateness of trees as subject matter for Black poets, Brooks informs him that Chicago poets
have been debating that very point. Her definitive response is
"certainly a black poet my be involved in a concern for trees,
if only because when he looks at one he thinks of how his

ancestors have been lynched thereon" (*Report from Part One* 166). Thus, her answer is "mediated by a communal consciousness and impulse arising from group sensibility."

On this point, Ron Baxter Miller brings his insight. He finds that even when Brooks' character is a male, as in "still do I keep my look, my identity" her character is as one with him as a product of shared realities. Miller cites "heredity and environment" in Brooks' work. Although Miller's drift seems to be a *universal everyman,* rather than an ethnic specific *every[black]man [woman],* the case he makes for this poem gets to the gist, too, of *Maud Martha.* Says Miller,

> In general the poem associates a soldier's personal or individual style with the invariant self that appears regardless of social class or life's experiences . . . the self does become visible in forms and situations as different as baseball and school . . . . In thinking of her own life-style, the narrator values his. (*A Life Distilled* 107)

Miller's remarks bring amplification to a reading of *Maud Martha,* in its perspective of an artist rooted in community, however wide her appeal.

Brooks' own verve that evinces regional Chicago, by that very aspect, brings attention to its African centeredness. Thus what is familiar about this author to other African centered people can be gleaned also in the writings of such authors as Ama Ata Aidoo (Ghana), Gayle Jones (USA-Lexington, KY), Nancy Morejon (Cuba), Paula Marshall (Barbados-USA), Lorraine Hansberry (USA, Chicago), Flora Nwapa (Nigeria), Nikky Finney (USA, North Carolina), Awa Thiam (Mali), Carolina Maria De Jesus (Brazil), and Bessie Head (South Africa) to name just a few remarkable Black women over time and across the globe. In *Daughters of Africa: An International*

Anthology of Words and Writings by Women of African Descent From the Ancient Egyptian to the Present, editor Margaret Busby brings together most of these and many others, and had no doubt to leave out as many more, plus some, due to the limited capacity of a single volume anthology.

Most pertinent to my essay, Busby begins her introduction to *Daughters of Africa* with a full copy of Gwendolyn Brook's poem "To Black Women." In this poem that begins with giving the word "Sisters" a line of its own, Brooks' hardy resound is "Prevail/. . . . And you create and train your flowers still." Remarkably, Busby immediately follows Brooks' poem with a quote from Maria W. Stewart that urges "O, ye daughters of Africa . . . Show forth to the world that ye are endowed with noble and exalted faculties"(xxix)—a quote which beyond the grave evokes that regal quality in the likes of the Maud Marthas of this world.

While *Maud Martha's* unique appeal transcends regional boundaries, it is about a Chicago girl come in to her womanhood. Anyone who grew up in Chicago, in the vicinity of the years in which Maud Martha grew up, give or take thirty years, before or after her young adulthood as recreated in the novel, knows experientially the physical, spiritual, geographical, social, and attitudinal region in which Maud Martha contends with life. Chicago's proud southside is on display here. It is not New York's historical Renaissance chic Harlem attitude; nor spread out L.A.'s Watts, in all its righteous rioting. Nor is it Detroit's Black Bottom risen to Motown fame. Rather, *Maud Martha* is a Chicago story, even though as explained, Maud Martha brings to mind many a woman almost anywhere in Africa or throughout the African Diaspora.

In Chicago, Black people watch their backs when outside the race-defined territories—just as if the whole outside was Marquette Park and they were Martin Luther King on a nonviolent march through. They also watch their backs within the race defined Black territories. A case can be make that to grow from birth through the teenage years on the South Side of Chicago, is to be exposed to sets of circumstances that amount to a kind of Basic Training for life. This training can prepare a person for whatever any part of Chicago, or the USA, or other parts of the world throws at her or him. One assessment of Maud Martha's preparation can be gleaned in a description of her thus: "Maud Martha's sensibility seems unthreatened" and "especially fitted" (Kent, *A Life of Gwendolyn Brooks* 116). She is fitted by family upbringing: by the security of parents' and siblings' love that helps her contend with their shortcomings. She is fitted by her "people everywhere . . . thronging 47th Street in Chicago..." (Margaret Walker qtd. in Busby 267). She is fitted by her people's affronts, yes, but equally so by "their variousness their ingenuity/their elan vital and that some thing essence/quiddity i cannot penetrate or name" (Robert Hayden 60).

During his 1967 interview with Brooks, Paul M. Angle pushes the question of environment: "So the human environment in which you lived has contributed to your poetry and has not affected it adversely." Brooks replies, "No, indeed, it hasn't affected it adversely, but helped me" (*Report from Part One* 134). But seemingly perplexed by this affirmation, Angle returns to this focus on the "human" environment of Brooks' Black Chicago, now coming out and naming the place, as if not fully satisfied yet with what he has been given on that point of gnawing preoccupation. Angle persists: "I suppose what I'm trying to lead up to is this question: Is the Chicago environment conducive to a writing career? Or does it have any effect on you one way or the other?" (135). Although ostensibly inquiring about whether Chicago affects her work, his "one way or the other" betrays his seeming assumption about the Chicago in which Brooks is situated. She informs him that she has always lived in Chicago, and though once curious as a child about the idyllic country life, she says, "I feel . . . that it was better for me to have grown up in Chicago because in my writing I am proud to feature people and their concerns—their troubles as well as their joys. The city is a place to observe man en masse and in his infinite variety"(135). Brooks says in this interview that she writes about the happenings all about her, what she sees and hears in the neighborhood. Says Leopold Sedar Senghor, the renowned African poet: "The traditional African narrative is woven [similarly] out of everyday life. . . . All the events become images and so acquire paradigmatic value and point beyond the moment" (qtd. in Obiechina 125).

Despite Brooks' decisive answer, the inquisition continues in an almost incredulous tone on the part of the interviewer:

> **Angle:** And this city furnishes you an environment which you find entirely satisfactory as far as your own career is concerned.
> It does not impede you...in any way?
> **Brooks:** It nourishes.
> **Angle:** So you would have no desire to . . . head off to New York?
> **Brooks:** No, I intend to live in Chicago for my forever. (135–136)

That in the very next breath Paul Angle asks Gwendolyn Brooks if she thinks she is handicapped by the fact that she is "a Negro" (*Report from Part One* 136), reveals the tracks along which this line of questioning runs. It shows him curious about her affinity for race and region. The benefit of such pointed inquiry is that in pushing for satisfaction to the questions on his mind, he makes known the thoughts of like-minded readers of Brooks, and thus of the everyday extraordinary Black women they encounter in passing. The benefit to my paper here is the interviewer's garnering of evidence of the importance of Chicago to *Maud Martha* as a place with a unique group of people—people connected to Blacks globally, yes, but particularly to Blacks throughout the USA. On this point of place, however, it is important to keep in mind the author's response to George Stavros' question: "Do you try to evoke place in your work?" (*Report from Part One* 161). Brooks, replies, "No, I start with people. For instance, Maud Martha goes to the Regal Theater, which is almost dead now, but had a great history in Chicago. She looks at the people; she looks at the star; she looks at the people coming out of the theater. But suffice it to say I don't start with the landmarks" (161).

On June 11, 2000 at Genesis Baptist Church in Greensboro, North Carolina, the Reverend Helen McLaughlin, Co-Pastor delivered "The Preached Word" (*Order of Worship* bulletin cover) in which her theme on from "scattered" to "gathered" provoked thought on how one moves from an aggrieved state to that calm which gives one that "peace which passes all understanding." Reverend Helen McLaughlin's sermon has implications for our understanding of Gwendolyn Brooks' novel *Maud Martha*. Whether at a beauty shop or formal ball, Maud Martha experiences crude insensitivity. On impact she suffers an internal scattering effect. This leaves her either incredulously doubting her ears when a white traveling saleswoman peddling cosmetics to black women invades the black beauty shop and casually uses the word nigger to describe a human workhorse; or when ostracized at a ball by her own husband who is sorry she is so dark, Maud Martha at first reacts to the crude insensitivity of her husband, thinking to take it out on the light-with-long-hair other woman: "go over there and scratch her upsweep down . . . spit on her back . . . scream." But then there is this moment of epiphany, and Maud Martha becomes (in Reverend McLaughlin's revelation) "gathered," for she realizes, "if the root is sour what business did she have up there hacking up a leaf?(88).

On the southside of Chicago one is environmentally raised (1) to expect to have things happen that on impact makes one feel internally scattered. Yet over the course of growing up, one becomes (2) astutely attuned to epiphanic discernment, for by that, one is able to (3) shift into a gathered gear, able to ease on into the next waiting scenario with all its ups and troubles. Such is the case with Maud Martha. Notes one reader, "The poet's own life-nourishing qualities define her heroine. Angers recede; rage glimmers and gleams, but sanity lights the path" (Melhem 87). In this essay I maintain that the vignettes reflect a personality formed by being scattered, by being attuned to epiphanic seizure, and thus gathered. Life of this sort does not construct an "ordinary" personality. Maud Martha, I argue, characteristic of other South Side Chicago women, is "extraordinary."

Thus, contrary to a popular reading of *Maud Martha,* this is not a story about a person who is ordinary, as any Black Chicago Southsider knows. Who there would call herself "ordinary" in the sense of that word's usual application to Black females by people whose angle of vision hits a blind spot when it comes to her specialness, her comeliness and her intelligence? However, for people who literally equate one's economic class and skin color with the word "ordinary" it may be necessary to return to basic dictionary study to discern the difference. My computerized *American Heritage Dictionary* defines "ordinary" thus : "1. Commonly encountered; usual." But I challenge: encountered by whom? Encountered, say, by David McKemster outside Mandel Hall on the University campus or by his chums Stickie and her beau Pat O'Brien? Encountered by the hat woman at the "millinery" shop?

Encountered by Mrs. Burns-Cooper? Encountered by "you old black gal" mouthing Emmanuel, kneeing his pick-up wagon? I wager a Chicagoan of the female persuasion on the South Side is not wont to turn over to the likes of these her own self-opinion. "Commonly encountered" puts the onus on the eyes of the beholder.

As regards the second dictionary meaning or "ordinary: 2.a. Of no exceptional ability, degree, or quality . . .; b. Of inferior quality; second-rate"—it is obvious that this bears no resemblance to Maud Martha. How are we to take the tendency to use this term by people who would never use a less evasive word to describe her—say not a curse word or racial slur—but instead this "ordinary" which is more apt to escape scrutiny. How is this business of "ordinary" personalized to Maud Martha? How is the term personalized to Gwendolyn Brooks? And how, I ask, is "ordinary" personalized to those millions of individual Black women who see some or a whole lot of themselves in the novel's heroine?

"Regal" ("magnificent; splendid") would be a more apt word to describe the character, the author, and the many visible Black women to whom she draws attention. Notice Brooks' splendid fun with the title of *"The Anniad."* An interviewer wants to know "What was behind the title in the first place? Is this a classical reference?" Brooks' answer is classic Chicago verve: "Well, the girl's name is Annie, and it was my little pompous pleasure to raise her to a height that she probably did not have. I thought of the *Iliad* and said, I'll call this *'The Anniad' (Report from Part One* 158).

Though encountered by people socialized to view Black skin and natural hair in a negative way, Maud Martha still enjoys "smiling beautifully to herself ("we're the only colored people here" 78). She will continue to go anywhere she wants to go, and in spite of the indifferent whites, will have herself a grand time, even. In the story we find her barely making her way to the exit through the theater lobby, yet already looking forward to the next time she and her hubby go uptown to (anthropologically) experience rich folks' treats. Quite naturally, being human, one is vulnerable to external forces of evil in life. When it happened in the life he knew, Jean Paul Sartre called it Existentialist despair (discussed in *Existentialism and Human Emotions*). A fearless commitment to astute awareness is what enables Black women like Maud Martha to enjoy that optimism that graces self-confidence.

Now, my argument here with the word "ordinary" is not enamored of petty semantically jockeying; rather my argument is infused by the desire to put into proper perspective the dangers of a seemingly casual word that may have no loaded denotations, but is loaded with a connotation of plain (at its most kindest) that is made manifest in how people are treated. The dark skinned girls and women of this world whose families might just happen to live on a really tight-to-meager budget, and whose names may be neither famous nor infamous, can not be assumed therefore to be "ordinary" in the manifested sense of that word as here explored. The white/light casting media who serve at the behest of the status quo are actually risking betraying themselves as "ordinary" (i.e. unattractive) in some regretful respect.

Too often, the word "ordinary" in the context in which I am proposing to revisit its caption of Maud Martha, can have a case made against it by showing it as analogous to the term "postcolonial" as challenged by Ama Ata Aidoo (who insists there is nothing post about colonialism):

> It could be argued that *postcolonial* offers a
> rational and neat construct in terms of liter-
> ary critique. But as we know all too well,
> literature and other forms of artistic expres-
> sion have an unruly way of not only reflecting

but also actively spilling into reality. Therefore,
those of us involved in the trade—whether
as writers or critics—have to exercise the most
extreme caution when we are bandying around
terminologies. (*Critical Fictions* 153)

Just as any Black Chicago Southsider with that certain verve and nerve, Maud Martha hardly looks upon herself as "common or ordinary." Immediate rejoinder to this statement abounds of course, using the narrator's own words. Many scholars have taken Brooks' own words to validate them on this, and in so doing, missing the point that Brooks never validates others' reading of her at her own expense. Maud herself makes the point at the onset of the novel in "description of Maud Martha," when identifying with dandelions. She says she likes their "demure prettiness second to their everydayness"(2) and that "it was hard to believe that a thing of ordinary allurement—if the allurement of any flower could be said to be ordinary—was as easy to love as a thing of heart-catching beauty"(2). The parenthetical "slap five" makes it clear that her seeming self-effacement more likely is a bold flaunting of her "prettiness." Black creators of "slap (or gimme) five" did so to physically punctuate a profundity in Black nuance. The fun element keeps at bay the stress, which the point is to reduce. Of course, the parenthetical spike in question can also be read as Black signifying in the jockeying sense of that game. Important here, is the fact that the parenthetical point takes a clever, light-hearted shot at the people who ignore what does not smack of white. Just because the narrator can *play* the devil's advocate with what she says about a dandelion *outside the parenthetical enclosure,* does not mean she would ever *seriously* become one against herself.

Problematically, references to Maud Martha's comparison of herself to a dandelion is used as proof of an assumed lowly aspect of her self- view. Harry B. Shaw in "War with Beauty" advances this reading. Speaking of Maud Martha, Shaw alleges,

> As she identified with the dandelion in Chapter
> I, 'Description of Maud Martha,' Maud expresses
> her basic need to be cherished. This chapter also
> lays the foundation for the struggle that occup-
> ies much of the novel. The struggle to feel
> cherished while knowing she was plain 'was the
> dearest wish of Maud Martha Brown.'
> (*Gwendolyn Brooks* 171)

Concerns with this reading abound. First (as noted above) there is the utter omission of the comment made in parenthe-sis: i.e., "if the allurement of any flower could be said to be ordinary." Second, in Shaw's deduction, there is the assump-tion that Maud is struggling to "feel" cherished. Actually what scatters her in this regard throughout the novel, is not her own struggle to feel cherished, for she is blessed with self-worth. What she struggles with is her disappointment in others who cannot win their bouts with internalized disdain of dark skin. If they could only feel about her as she feels about herself, her loved ones and acquaintances would reap the full benefit of their relationship with her. Corroborating evidence for this reading is to be found in Patricia Hill Collins' sense of the matter. Collins' diagnosis of Maud Martha's husband finds "his inability to 'jump away up high' over the wall of color limited his ability to fully appreciate his wife" (*Black Feminist Thought* 82). Yet, *his* inability does not interfere with Maud's ability to fully appreciate herself. This is hard for some peo-ple to believe. According to Shaw, "Although she thinks the dandelion is pretty, she is aware that others consider it plain or ugly—a weed" (*A Life Distilled* 257). This problem with believing a Black woman cannot really think that she is pretty, against the judgment of "others", is not just Shaw's problem but that of so many people who project onto Black women their own internalized befuddlement. However, Chicagoans for sure, but as certainly Black women all over world, won't sit still for this!

What blocks understanding for so many can perhaps be partly explained in our play with words that may need to be seriously examined for the unintentional backfire. Given the way Black people pay backhand compliments to oppressors in our use of such psychologically empowering constructions as *the man* and *Miss Ann*, or present-day references to enslavers as masters and mistresses, it is no wonder that Maud Martha's hugely adroit self-appreciation, is read by Shaw as "inferiority (173) or sour grapes"(165). Many people are just too far from reading a Black skinned woman as anything other than how American has publicized her projected morale since the time that Black people gained physical manumission. We have been told so often that she has an inferiority complex, that some refuse to believe on a gut level that she does not, even when mouthing the politically expedient opposite. Maud Martha's sense of self-worth is so exquisitely sober, that a certain kind of person is apt to mistake her for an upstart, as does David McKemster. Her nerve to come to Hyde Park is an affront to his great fun passing time with whites. While it behooves him to act civil and invite her for refreshments and see her to the bus stop, David McKemster is at pains to do so and in his very coolness attempts to lord it over her—especially when he is showing off to impress white friends. Given that David McKemster once visited Maud for woe-unto-me intellectual venting, the reader is not at all amused at his standoffishness in "an encounter." Patricia Hills Collins has scrutinized this sort of fallout which is shown to occur "when a hierarchy of any kind invades interpersonal relationships among individuals, and the actual consciousness of individuals themselves" (165).

But Brooks, herself, has pinned her own mantel to her own breast. It might be okay to conjecture here that she has primped her comeliest charms before her bedroom mirror. Thus, as Brooks finds herself utterly desirable, she has the confidence to see a man from across a crowded room (for the first time) and on the spot tell her good friend Margaret, "I am going to marry that man." In marrying the man of her choice, Maud Martha, then, is hardly a woman who lets others' socio/psychological limitations deter her from sharing what she knows a good man could admire until death.

From the onset of the novel—if one reads selectively for the positive—it is clear that Maud Martha is confident enough to come right out and admire her "demur prettiness" by way of admiration for a flower. If we ponder the problem that modesty and decorum poses for coming right out and saying what one likes—i.e. what one feels—about oneself, we can all the more admire the delicate route Maud Martha takes by way of a flower to get there. For Heaven's sake, she would have been boasting to select a rose.

Maud Martha has a well-balanced ego under her own control. The narrator's poetic conceit would not select a cliché rose anyway. Maud Martha, then, uses a ploy of the other extreme: understatement. This is something a Black woman uses at risk of seeming to lack self-assurance. Because our society allows a Kevin Costner to strategically self-efface in the process of self-promoting, he is not taken literally when he does so. The same is true for a Sharon Stone. The same is true for Vanessa Williams and Lena Horne. But do not let Cicely Tyson strategically self-efface her beauty in order to celebrate her "demure prettiness," or she, like a lot of us and Maud Martha, will be comforted with a Hallmark word of condolence. Clearly, a person's reaction has to do with how he or she feels about a dark skinned Black woman whose countenance is free of European features (from hair to nose). Clearly, Maud Martha favors her dark brown skin and other physical charms along with her mind. Brooks' Maud Martha, recalls Zora Neale Hurston's expression of feeling sorry for anyone who lacked the ability to appreciate her fine self. Brooks' parenthesis is a contradiction to what's outside of it; it is not intended to be ignored, any more than the novel's star. She should be seen and heard in the way intended. Barbara Christian points out that "although the substance of the novel is told through Maud Martha's eyes, Brooks suggests, by her use of the objective third person, that other eyes see what hers see" and that Maud Martha "is solidly located in a world of many others" (138).

Of course Shaw is joined by a host of other respected scholars who quote the dandelion story, choosing also to omit the crucial material highlighted (as opposed to tucked away) in parenthesis. Sometimes quotation marks signal the scholar's awareness that the word has a problematic rub in reference to Black females, as when Paula Giddings writes: "Gwendolyn Brooks's Maud Martha brought to the fore the first 'ordinary' female protagonist" (*When and Where I Enter* 255). I am not suggesting that the word "ordinary" as applied to Maud Martha, thus to Black women similarly endowed, intentionally patronizes. Rather, I am suggesting that Black women, long abused by neglect as well as blatant attack, tend to scrutinize how language effects behavior when it comes to what they grant others the right to call them. Barbara Christian, though reverting to the word ordinary several times in "Nuance and the Novella," clarifies the reading of "ordinary" as "at least on the surface" (*Black Feminist Criticism* 129), thus indicating her awareness that "extraordinary" is more like it. More riveting than "ordinary," Shaw insists that [Maud Martha] is "lowly" (165). Lowly! I strongly disagree!

Third and finally, Shaw weaves together his words with
Brooks to effect the slant he takes on things, which I argue, are
contrary to her self-view. The lead-in to a quote must take
into account the great care a poet such as Brooks takes in
wording for conciseness of meaning. The word "plain" is a
stranger to Chapter 1 of *Maud Martha,* wherein we are given
"the description of Maud Martha." Here a dandelion is a
"jewel . . . studding the patched green dress of her back
yard"(2). The dandelions appeal to her because their "demure
prettiness . . . reminded her of herself"(2). The author, being
too well raised to brag, lets poetic license take a lyrical route to
her truth.

The tendency of critics to see Brooks as preoccupied with
color, misses the point of the novelist being the artist who
encourages us to pause and reflect on the world. Brooks is
among the many Black women writers who bring the skin
color/hair texture issue to the public's attention in their works.
In recreating in literature a phenomenon in society, a writer is
not to be assumed to have a personal obsession with the problem. The African tradition, unlike the European tradition,
invests literature with proverbial functions. In giving shape to
experiences, beyond mere entertainment or delight in acro-
batic language feats, creative writers give humans something
to ponder about actual life. According to Leopard Sedar
Senghor:

> stories function as proverbs in . . . oral discourse
> in African traditional societies, and are so readily
> assimilated within an extended written narrative
> form like the novel which explores life in terms
> of its functional and ethical values. Chinua
> Achebe, the foremost African novelist, is . . .
> emphatic in identifying the social and ethical
> significance of the story. (qt. in Obiechina 124)

Along this line of discussion, during his interview with Brooks, Stavros asks if she agrees with Ellison and Baldwin . . . "that the protest novel should be replaced by something less social"(160) to which Brooks definitively responds, "No. I don't feel that way at all"(160). She says that a person "should write out of his won milieu" and that she will "go right on writing about black people as people"(Stavros 163). One of the things Black people do is concern themselves with skin color.

In *Thomas and Beulah,* Rita Dove portrays the skin color concern in her poem "Taking in Wash," writing "She was Papa's girl,/black though she was"(47). In *Sister Outsider,* Audre Lorde wonders as a youngster:

> Somewhere I knew it was a lie that nobody
> else noticed color. Me darker than my two
> sisters . . . I was always jealous of my sisters
> because my mother thought they were such
> good girls, whereas I was bad. . . . Did bad
> mean Black ? The endless scrubbing with
> lemon juice in the cracks and crevices of my
> ripening, darkening, body. And oh, the sins
> of my dark elbows and knees, my gums and
> nipples, the folds of my neck and the cave
> of my armpits! (149)

In "The Butt of the Joke" dedicated to Karen Whoopi Goldberg Johnson" poet Nikky Finney muses, "You were the little girl on stage/made from different pieces of us all/a one woman show/mobile awning of melanin and goosedown lips/with a long wavy towel propped for false dreamy hair"(101). And in her autobiography *I Put A Spell On You,* Nina Simone writes:

> I wrote a song, 'Four Women', which went
> into these feelings a little. The women in the

song are black, but their skin tones range from light to dark and their ideas about beauty and their own importance are deeply influence by that. All the song did was to tell what entered the minds of most black women in America when they thought about themselves. (117).

Nina Simone was concerned that black women were being "defined by things they didn't control and until they had the confidence to define themselves they'd be stuck in the same mess forever—that was the point of the song" (117). However, after the song was released in 1966, some black radio programs thought it insulted Black women and refused to play it. Says Simone, "banning it was a stupid thing to do. The song told a truth that many people in the USA—especially black men—simply weren't ready to acknowledge at that time"(117). Taking an historical look at the skin color in Black history Paula Giddings finds:

> There is little question that a color-consciousness of the self-hate variety was at work. But it wasn't the only thing at work. Because of historical circumstances as much as attitude, fair complexions were associated with upper classes. Black with White forebears usually had more educational and economic opportunities, were more easily accepted, and thus made up a disproportionate number of achievers. Of the 131 men and 8 women listed in W.E.B. Du Bois's *Who's Who of Colored Americans,* published in 1916, for example, 124 of the men and all of the women were of mixed heritage. (*When and Where I Enter* 186)

Clearly, Brooks' *Maud Martha* brings attention to an obsession that touches all periods and eras of America—from the neo television casting that prefers light black, back to the cotton clubs, and white supper clubs that insisted on light complexioned dancers who would not offend the appetites of their white patrons. But Maud Martha does not judge herself harshly simply because others have a difficult time with her features. Given the body of work attesting to Black women's positive view of themselves, it is difficult to understand why so many people have a hard time believing Maud Martha when she tells us she likes her "demur prettiness."

The Wayan brothers horridly miscued mockery of Venus and Serena Williams, (which is more of their thinly disguised racial self-denigration trying to pass as funny) is just one recent glaring attack on the black skinned and limbed all American girl. The sisters will no more let these men confound their game, their winning streak, than will Maud Martha let "Paul at the 011 Club" destroy her. She, like the sisters, bring astute attention to the business at hand. The Williams sisters' strength of bearing and Afrocentric grooming attest to the acclaim they feel when they look into the mirror. In her poem "To A Dark Girl" Gwendolyn Bennet muses confidently, "Keep all you have of queenliness/Forgetting that you were once a slave/And let your full lips laugh at Fate" (Busby 216). Thus just as there are the attacks on blackness in jingles such as the one which ends "If you are black, get back" there are equally enticing jingles of the opposite note such as "The blacker the berry the sweeter the juice." As far back as the 1700s Phillis Wheatley referred to black in the positive imagery of "sable." In the 1800s Sojourner Truth set people straight about just who she was, and that was *some extraordinarily terrific* woman. From Jamaica, Una Marson (1905-1965) composed "Kinky Hair Blues," which, like Maud Martha, laments others' hang-ups with a black girls looks but emphasizes:

> I like me black face
> And me kinky hair
> I like me black face
> And me kinky hair (Busby 222)

Here, Maud Martha's voice is evoked when out on the town content within the confines of her own fine Black frame, she is yet left to sit sizzling with anger watching her husband play the dandy with "Gold Spangles" on the dance floor at Club 99. While Gayle Jones' little orphan Rena shows by her frown and striking the table that she is "impatient with his ignorance" ("Ravena" 1835), when a man who has connected with her, and should know better, allows her to be rejected in favor of another orphan on the basic of lightness of skin color, Maud Martha talks herself out of taking it out on "Gold Spangles, reasoning "if the root was sour what did she have up there hacking at a leaf?" (*Maud Martha* 88).

A self-sustaining legacy positions Black women to "bring noble understanding" (*Maud Martha* 35) to the shortcomings of others who figure importantly in their lives. It is the legacy passed on by Mari E. Evans when she sings praises of the black woman "tall as cypress/strong/beyond all definition still/defying place/ and time/ and circumstance/ assailed/ impervious/ indestructible/ look/ on me and be/ renewed (Busby 300). Gwendolyn Brooks is of this mold and her own character reads through in her novel *Maud Martha.* In *and they didn't die* the South African author Lauretta Ngcobo dedicates her book to her mother thus: "To my mother . . . who by example taught me to cope and to straddle contradictions, and who above all believes in me." This dedication also recalls Brooks' mentoring mother who surely figures in Brooks' ability to empower her autobiographical heroine, Maud Martha, with a good rapport with self.

As stated at the onset of this paper, Maud Martha is a regal and regional personality. Living on the southside of Chicago, she daily evinces an exquisite self-assuredness that places her firmly in a literary reality of self-appreciating Black women. In the novel's sardonic treatment of the people whose hedonistic arrogance begs to be put in place, Gwendolyn Brooks compels readers to free themselves of their own ordinary approach to Black women, and see the dandelion for her beauty and clever stroke of genius.

Work Cited

Aidoo, Ama Ata. "Conference Presentation." *Critical Fictions: The Politics of Imaginative Writings.* Ed. Philomena Mariani. Seattle: Bay Press, 1991.

Brooks, Gwendolyn. 1953. *Maud Martha.* Chicago: Third World Press, 1993.

Brooks, Gwendolyn. *Report From Part One.* Detroit: Broadside Press, 1973.

Busby, Margaret. *Daughters of Africa.* New York: Pantheon Books, 1992.

Collins, Patricia Hill. *Black Feminist Thought: Knowledge, Consciousness, and the Politics of Empowerment.* New York: Routledge, 1990.

Christian, Barbara. "Nuance and the Novella: A Study of Gwendolyn Brooks's *Maud Martha.*" *Black Feminist Criticism: Perspectives on Black Women Writers.* New York: Pergamon Press, 1985.

Christian, Barbara. *Black Feminist Criticism.* New York: Pergamon Press, 1985.

Dove, Rita. "Taking in Wash." *Thomas and Beulah.* Pittsburgh: Carnegie-Mellon University Press, 1986

Finney, Nikky: "The Butt of the Joke." *Rice.* Toronto, Ontario: Sister Vision, 1995.

Giddings, Paula. *When and Where I Enter: The Impact of Black Women on Race and Sex in America.* New York: Quill, William Morrow, 1984.

Jones, Gayle. "Ravenna." *Call and Response.* Gen. Ed. Patricia Liggins Hill et al.. New York: Houghton Mifflin, 1998. 1832–1835.

Jordan, June. "Who Look At Me" *Naming Our Destiny.* New York: Thunder's Mouth Press, 1989

Kent, George. "Aesthetic Values in the Poetry of Gwendolyn Brooks." *A Life Distilled: Gwendolyn Brooks, Her Poetry and Fiction.* Eds. Maria K. Mootry and Gary Smith. Urbana: University of Illinois Press, 1987.

Kent, George E. A Life of Gwendolyn Brooks. Lexington:The University Press of Kentucky, 1990.

Lee, Don L. Preface. *Report from Part One..* Gwendolyn Brooks. Detroit: Broadside Press, 1973.

Lorde, Audre. "Eye to Eye:Black Women Hatred and Anger." *Sister Outsider.* Freedom, California: The Crossing Press, 1984.

Melhem, D.H. Gwendolyn Brooks: *Poetry and the Heroic Voice.* The University Press of Kentucky: Lexington, 1987. Miller, Ron Baxter. "Does Man Love Art." *A Life Distilled: Gwendolyn Brooks Her Poetry and Fiction.* Eds. Marie Mootry and Gary Smith. Urbana: University of Illinois Press, 1987.

Mootry, Marie and Smith, Gary, eds. *A Life Distilled: Gwendolyn Brooks, Her Poetry and Fiction.* Urbana: University of Illinois Press, 1987.

Ngcobo, Lauretta. *And They Didn't Die.* New York: Feminist Press at the City University of New York, 1995.

Obiechina, Emmanuel. "Narrative Proverbs in the African Novel." *Research in African Literature* 24.4 (1993): 123. (18??)

Shaw, B. Harry. *Gwendolyn Brooks.* Boston: Twayne Publishing, 1980.

Simone, Nina. *I Put A Spell On You. New York:* DeCapo Press, 1993.

Four

The Aliveness of Things:
Nature in *Maud Martha*

Larry R. Andrews

In her autobiographical *Report from Part One,* Gwendolyn Brooks concludes her "marginalia" comments concerning *Maud Martha* with the statement that she is "interested in the fact that the first passage I wrote of this novel I did not use until I reached the opening of the last chapter, 'back from the wars!'" Was she interested only in the seeming paradox that the germ of the novel ended up coming near its very end? Because she follows this comment with a full quotation of the third and fourth paragraphs of that last chapter, we might infer that she is also intent on emphasizing this passage as central to the novel.

The final chapter does in fact offer a climactic statement of what seems to be the main theme of the work: the persistence of a life force amid instability and destruction. It connects this force of nature to Maud Martha's personal sense of vitality: the bright sunshine "glorifying every bit of her room" and the air "like a feather" evoke in her a euphoric moment; the air "made her sit up in bed and stretch, and zip the dark green shade up to the very top of the window—and made her whisper, What, what, am I to do with all of this life?" (RPO 193, *Maud Martha* 320). In the finished novel, Brooks contextualizes this seed-image of the novel with the end of World War II and the return of "Peace" and Maud's brother Harry. As the chapter moves from Maud's expansive relief and her sense of the life-power within her to a generalized statement about regeneration, it places this optimism in the sobering context of the maimed bodies of the soldiers and the news of lynchings in the

South. Nevertheless, "the sun was shining, and some of the people in the world had been left alive, and it was doubtful whether the ridiculousness of man would ever completely succeed in destroying the world." The force of the dandelion returning in the spring is irrepressible, as is the daily "glorious and brave" struggle of ordinary people. The cycle of the chapter returns to Maud, who is expecting another baby. She is bid "bon voyage" by the weather—an anticipation of the energetic adventures Brooks speaks of in the planned sequel, as reported in her interview "Update on *Part One*" (Hull and Gallagher).

I want to return to this final chapter later, but what interests me is how this germ idea for a book about a "black girl growing up in Chicago" (Stavros 17) in the 1930s and 1940s can help us understand the tensions and conflicts in the novel in the light of a positive world view in which the author and protagonist are closely attuned to nature. As Brooks emphasizes in *In the Mecca,* written soon after this novel, the statement "Conduct your blooming in the noise and whip of the whirlwind" suggests that we can take comfort in our ability to resist disorder and suffering:

> The world is a whirlwind. . . . Do we tell ourselves that we'll wait until it's all over and everything is peaceful and loving? We might be waiting in vain. We don't know when things are going to quotes "get better"—and we don't seem inclined to force them to be better. So we see to it that we bloom, that we attend to our growth in spite of the awful things that are happening. (Hull and Gallagher 39)

Using this nature image, Brooks asserts that we have power to grow, to resist victimization, to become responsible, despite forces of oppression and destruction. Barbara Christian has noted the centrality of Maud's question, "What, what am I to do with all of this life?" but treats it as both the universal question of how we are to live our lives and how a black girl of that time and place could live given her limitations of opportunity (246-247). I suggest that the "life" Maud intuits refers not to her lifespan or career but to a life force of nature to which she is attuned, and that it gives her a source of personal power akin to the personal power Hermine's cowboy uncles advise her to find in Linda Beatrice Brown's recent *Crossing Over Jordan.* D. H. Melhem refers to Maud's question as expressing the "essence of youth," but she also refers to her "Wordsworthian 'natural piety'" and the insight she draws about herself from "contemplating nature." I want to emphasize and extend her interpretation of this sense of nature in Maud's world view.

Mary Helen Washington has recognized the potential personal power in Maud's anger but finds it silenced. Although she agrees that in the final chapter Maud is "exhilarated and full of energy" and that her pregnancy is "a powerful way-of-being in the world" ("For, in the midst of destruction and death, she will bring forth life"), she ultimately finds problematic Maud's unresolved, silent anger (465-466). I want to suggest that Maud's sense of her own aliveness and the aliveness of things in the outside world is the source of both her anger and her joy, of both her heightened sensitivity and her resilience. Patricia and Vernon Lattin argue amply and well for Maud Martha's ability to "combine a subtle cynicism with a genuine acceptance of the human condition" (142) through a "dual vision that allows her to see simultaneously beauty in ugliness, life in death, and a positive way of living by which one can maintain one's self-respect and creativity in the face of overwhelmingly negative forces" (137). I find the energy source for this ability not just in Maud's complex personality

color and nature

but in her connectedness to nature.

This positive sense of being part of nature differs from a facile optimism or, in socio-political terms, the integrationist philosophy of the 1950s some critics have used to characterize Brooks's supposedly pre-militant and pre-womanist period. We might call it a "pragmatic optimism" rooted in the ordinary and concrete. In the novel it is reflected in a variety of ways. First, Maud's responsiveness to details of color and texture reflects not only an artistic sensibility, as Washington and others have noted, but a sense of biological and intuitive connectedness to nature. Second, Brooks's use of personifications and other tropes that mingle animal and human, animate and inanimate, conveys Maud's sense of living in a dynamic universe in which everything seems alive, full of movement and change. Third, in direct descriptions of nature Brooks threads her portrayal of an urban ghetto with a surprising life force. Fourth, Brooks imbues Maud with unusual vitality and life-fostering power. Finally, even anger, suffering, and death can be understood in the framework of resilience, growth, and survival.

Almost every critic has mentioned the "lyrical" or "impressionistic" quality of the novel, usually referring to concrete images as well as to rhythm, diction, and tone. Mary Helen Washington aptly counters the blitheness of many of the early characterizations of this sort: "What the reviewers saw as exquisite lyricism was actually the truncated stuttering of a woman whose rage makes her literally unable to speak" (453). But she also acknowledges that the whole novel reflects the sensibility of an artist, saying that Maud Martha "perceives the world sensuously, she responds to the complexity of beauty"; though not allowed by Brooks to become an artist per se, she nevertheless exhibits the language, memory, insight, imagination, and honesty of the artist (458). I would argue that Maud Martha's responsiveness to beauty and texture reveals not only an aesthetic sensibility but also a sense of connectedness and openness to nature, thus differentiating it from, for example, Helga Crane's love of color and style in Nella Larsen's *Quicksand.* The emphasis on color evokes life vividly, while grayness evokes death, stasis, the forces arrayed against life. In Chapter 2 the school children become "[b]its of pink, of blue, white, yellow, green, purple, brown, black, carried by jerky little stems of brown or yellow or brown-black, [which] blew by the unhandsome gray and decay of the double-apartment buildings" (147). House interiors abound in color. Her childhood bedroom has "red draperies with white and green flowers" and a "dresser with blue paper flowers" (149). Her and Paul's first apartment has green wallpaper "with little red fishes swimming about" (203). On the other hand, her plans to make green the dominant color and create a cheerful, life-nourishing space are muted by the owner's rules about making changes and by the dominant color of gray associated with the miserable human lives in the kitchenette building: "The color was gray, and the smell and sound had taken on a suggestion of the properties of color, and impressed one as gray, too. . . . There was a whole lot of grayness here" (205-206).

Maud's rich fantasies of elegance and grace exude color and fine textures. To eighteen-year-old Maud, New York meant "the bristling or the creamy or the tactfully shimmering ways of life," "rooms with wood paneling, softly glowing, touched up by the compliment of a spot of auburn here, the low burn of a rare binding there . . . bits of dreamlike crystal; a taste of leather" (190), "little diamond-shaped cheeses that paprika had but breathed on" and "velvet-lined impossible shops" (191), voices with "fur at the base" and a Japanese screen "with rich and mellow, bread-textured colors" (192-193). She loved "to dwell upon color and soft bready textures and light, on a complex beauty, on gemlike surfaces" (193). At the cinema with Paul, she imagines returning to "a sweet-smelling apartment with flowers on little gleaming tables; and wonderful silver on night-blue velvet, in chests; and crackly sheets; and lace spreads on such beds as you saw at Marshall Field's" instead of the "kit'n't apt., with the garbage of your floor's families in a big can just outside your door, and the gray sound of little gray feet scratching away from it" (219). Balancing realistically her sensuous fantasies again are the gray realities of tenement life and the gray descriptions associated with the deaths of her grandmother and her uncle Tim.

Given the sparseness of narration, the plenitude of detail is all the more striking. Brooks dwells fondly on descriptions of clothes, of food, of the decor for the Dawn Ball, of the interior of the 011 Club, of family traditions. In several striking instances, she presents concrete details at the ends of chapters to shift the tone or comment ironically on the scene that has just taken place. For example, at the end of Chapter 24, "an encounter," which satirizes painfully her former beau David McKemster's need for approval by intellectual whites, she ironically undercuts the phony conversation by ending the scene abruptly with a single-sentence paragraph seemingly neutral in its reportage but symbolically evoking white culture: "The waitress brought coffee, four lumps of sugar wrapped in pink paper, hot mince pie" (275). At the end of the "millinery" chapter, in which Maud has gained a satisfying, if a bit mean-spirited, revenge against the racism of white shopkeepers, the parting paragraph portrays the saleswoman talking to her hats after having been left in the lurch by Maud: "Black-oh, black-: said the hat woman to her hats-which, on the slender stands, shone pink and blue and white and lavender, showed off their tassels, their sleek satin ribbons, their veils, their flower coquettes" (299). The loving description of the hats imbues them with an innocence and joy of life missing from the politics of the human encounter, as if to say, "This is what life should really be about, this beauty, in a world without racism, classism, and the games of power that people play."

Finally, at the end of Chapter 30, "at the Burns-Coopers'," the narrator asserts Maud's calm determination not to put up with the paternalistic racism of her employers-for-a-day: "Why, one was a human being. One wore clean nightgowns. One loved one's baby. One drank cocoa by the fire-or the gas range-come the evening, in the wintertime" (305). Using ordinary detail from daily life to define the concept of "human being," Brooks makes a quietly understated point rather than a dramatic statement of outrage. Although one may question Maud's refusal to confront Mrs. Burns-Cooper—because she is convinced that explanation would be futile—Maud has learned much from this brief stint as a maid about her husband Paul's daily suffering from racist indignities on the job and about her own mature ability to cope with them in her own way. This method is to survive through the strength Maud draws from the very aliveness of those mundane details listed. Commenting on the same passage, Annette Oliver Shands says that "the essence of being human has to do with attending to one's human needs-the needs that sustain life" (26).

It is a tribute to Maud's character that she can transcend several problematic issues associated with her aesthetic sensibility. Her fantasies about elegance, grace, and high style, for example, betray consumerist influences, class status issues, and white standards of beauty of those and later times. Buffeted by racism and colorism and convinced of her "dark" ugliness, she grows an appetite fed by magazines, advertisements, and movies. Yet early on, she accommodates pragmatically to her social and economic limitations while maintaining that lively response to beauty so evident still in the final chapter. Thus her sensuous perceptions are ultimately uncontaminated by classism and racism. Another problem is voiced by

Washington—Why isn't Maud allowed to fulfill her cravings for artistic form by becoming an artist, as Brooks herself had? (459). Whether because of the limits of the times or the frequent practice of women writers to "make their first woman protagonist a homebody" (Washington 459, citing Paule Marshall), Maud herself has, after considering an artistic medium, finally concluded that cultivating herself is the best thing for her:

> What she wanted was to donate to the world
> a good Maud Martha. That was the offering,
> the bit of art, that could not come from any
> other. She would polish and hone that. (164)

This conscious commitment is a choice of life as art or life over art, but clearly a choice to affirm life in its very essence. This essence can be lived only in the concrete details. When critics note the theme of "ordinariness" in the novel (e.g., Christian 241), they sometimes underestimate the elevated role Brooks gives ordinary detail by connecting it to the life force of nature.

The connection between human beings and nature becomes clearer in a number of tropes that mingle the two. Some of these personify the inanimate, making it come alive. In various whimsical passages, the sun "was making little silver promises somewhere up there, hinting" (146), the door is "friendly" and the iron fence "emphatic" (170), and "the very finest bits of white powder [of snow were] coming down with an almost comical little ethereal hauteur, to add themselves to the really important, piled-up masses of their kind" (214). In the context of the white boy Charles' visit and Maud's vulnerability, empty chairs seem human: "Three or four straight chairs that had long ago given up the ghost of whatever shallow dignity they may have had in the beginning and looked completely disgusted with themselves and with the Brown family" (158). In Maud's world, china can sit "in cheerful dignity" (248) and color can be "sleepy" (291).

Other figures interchange the natural and human worlds. Paulette's insides are "scampering like mice" (314), and eyes can have "metal" in them (292) as well as "diamonds and stars" (314). The opening "demure" dandelions are "[y]ellow jewels for everyday, studding the patched green dress of her back yard," and Maud compares this flower reassuringly to herself:

> she thought she saw a picture of herself, and
> it was comforting to find that what was
> common could also be a flower. . . .
>   . . . it was hard to believe that a thing of
> only ordinary allurements—if the allurements
> of any flower could be said to be ordinary—
> was as easy to love as a thing of heart-catching
> beauty.
> Such was her sister Helen! (144)

The following chapter expands the flower metaphor to the school children, who are merged with the wind as well: "Up the street, mixed in the wind, blew the children. . . . Bits of pink, of blue, white, yellow, green, purple, brown, black, carried by jerky little stems . . . ." (147). Later, again, people are "blooming" on Thirty-fourth Street: "It was August, and Thirty-fourth Street was all in bloom. The blooms, in their undershirts, sundresses and diapers, were hanging over porches and fence stiles and strollers, and were even bringing chairs out to the rims of the sidewalks" (306). Maud concludes from this picture of the black community in its daily ordinariness that life is largely comedy, not tragedy. Ongoing survival as a value is linked to the ongoing life and growth in nature.

Direct descriptions of nature insinuate themselves constantly in the urban setting of the novel so as to assert a living
presence and source of power. In the opening, Maud "chiefly
saw" the dandelions, but she also reports "the west sky, so
altering" and the imagined "meadow" that "made her breathe
more deeply, and either fling her arms or want to fling her
arms, depending on who was by, rapturously up to whatever
was watching in the sky" (143-144). The very opening chapter thus places Maud in the context of nature, and in an open
and ecstatic posture, and links to it her intimate sense of herself as a common dandelion. Later she pauses to note a gray
sky (146), the force of the wind (147), and the "little plots of
dirt and scanty grass that held up their narrow brave banners:
PLEASE KEEP OFF THE GRASS-NEWLY SEEDED"—
germs of life struggling to survive just as the "tiny lives" are
thrusting forth their energy amid the "cramp, inhibition, and
choke" of the ghetto (147). When her own family is threat-
ened with dispossession, it is not only the house that Maud
will dearly miss but also its natural setting, which includes a
poplar tree, a snake plant, an "obstinate slip" of fern, and "the
late afternoon light on the lawn" (170). Echoing Brooks's own
childhood infatuation with the sky (*RPO* 55), Maud perceives
the sky as unique to their house: "[S]he felt that the little line
of white, somewhat ridged with smoked purple, and all that
cream-shot saffron, would never drift across any western sky
except that in back of this house. The rain would drum with
as sweet a dullness nowhere but here" (172).

Nature is densely interwoven with the life and hopes of the
family, reflecting values of place and "rootedness" that Brooks
also cherished while writing the novel for the purpose of secur-
ing a down payment on a first house for her own family (Kent
104). The remarkable snowball bush also anchors Maud
Martha: "The snowballs had been so beautiful, so fat and star-
tlingly white in the sunlight, that she had suddenly loved

home a thousand times more than ever before, and had not wanted to go [on the trip] to Milwaukee" (229). Because the bush gradually sickened and died ("Each year the snowballs were smaller and more dispirited."), however, the memory aptly reflects the troubled context of disillusionment in which she recalls it—Paul's flirtation with Maella at the Dawn Ball.

Maud's compassionate sparing of the mouse she has trapped and her difficulties cleaning a chicken bespeak her sense that these animals are related to human beings. She whimsically imagines a little mouse family, with children named Betty and Bobby, living in hardship and worrying about education. Only the shortages of World War II enable her to fight the "nasty, nasty mess" of the chicken, but here, too, she imagines the chicken as a human being. Comic as the scene is, it affirms a central value for Maud:

> And yet the chicken was a sort of person, a
> respectable individual, with its own kind of
> dignity. The difference was in the knowing.
> What was unreal to you, you could deal with
> violently. If chickens were ever to be safe,
> people would have to live with them, and
> know them, see them loving their children,
> finishing the evening meal, arranging
> jealousy. (295)

Having been treated as "unreal" or "other" herself, Maud respects life in all its forms. In *Report from Part One*, Brooks says that the chapter

> is based on my old feelings regarding 'dressing'
> a chicken, and on my continuing feelings, that
> chickens are people, as are dogs, cats, rats, ants,
> birds, snakes, roaches, bears, fish, trees,

> weeds, flowers. People, that is, in the
> sense that we conceive people to be:
> things of identity and response. (193)

Nevertheless—and this is the life force too—"[when] the animal was ready for the oven Maud Martha smacked her lips at the thought of her meal"! (295).

The most abstract statement about nature comes in Chapter 21, "posts," in which Maud Martha considers how people "have to choose something decently constant to depend on, . . . to lean on" (242). Recognizing the fallibility of romantic love and even the "breadier love" in families and friendship, she posits: "Could be nature, which had a seed, or root, or an element (what do you want to call it) of constancy, under all that system of change" (243). The following chapter starts by referring to her search for "something solid. . . . shimmering form; warm, but hard as stone and as difficult to break," something she finds in tradition (244). In nature, expressed both in the natural order outdoors and in the stability of cyclically repeated family traditions, Maud finds a basis for her faith and optimism about the world. This optimism surges in the final chapter under the direct force of the sunlight and air, which "make" Maud respond with a sense of extraordinary personal power she can only call "life" (319-320). She returns to the image of the dandelion from the beginning and places it in the eternally recurring cycle of the seasons, giving it a power transcending the "ridiculousness of man" (321).

Maud Martha herself becomes a direct expression of nature through her life-giving power. Melhem declares that "the poet's own life-nourishing qualities define her heroine" (87). Maud's vitality of observation, reflection, and critique is pervasive, lending considerable liveliness to the text's limited omniscient narration. She easily recognizes vitality in others, such as neighbors Clement Lewy or the boisterous Viota, as well as false vitality, as in Howie Joe's shallow entertainment at the Regal. She feels a strong impulse to create, as mentioned earlier, which she applies to her own life. Her relations with animals are empathetic and life-supporting. Despite her deep disgust and disillusionment with the cockroaches and mice of her apartment, she releases a mouse she has captured and experiences a wave of capaciousness and virtue:

> Suddenly, she was conscious of a new cleanness
> in her. A wide air walked in her. A life had
> blundered its way into her power and it had been
> hers to preserve or destroy. She had not destroyed.
> In the center of that simple restraint was-creation.
> She had created a piece of life. It was wonderful.
> Why," she thought, as her height doubled, "Why,
> I'm good! I am good." (212-213)

The frequently claustral imagery of the book, the cramped stairs and small rooms set in opposition to the spaciousness of the images of nature, suddenly gives way. Maud Martha experiences a great swell of personal power by choosing to nourish life even in such a small event.

Maud's empathy underlines the lengthy Chapter 23, "kitchenette folks," with its finely drawn character sketches. The "insane" Binnie/Bennie's fondness for her confers recognition of her accepting nature. When she sees the soldiers returning from World War II "with two arms off and two legs off, the men with the parts of faces. Then her guts divided, then her eyes swam under frank mist" (320-321). In her resentment of her sister Helen's role as "favorite," Maud Martha tells us how she rescued her brother Harry from bullies and comforted her father:

who was it who sympathized with him in

humanity of empathy

his decision to remain, for the rest of his days,
the simple janitor! . . . Who was it who
sympathized with him in his almost desperate
love for this old house? Who followed him
about, emotionally speaking, loving this, doting
on that? (179-180).

wpt. scene

For husband Paul she is "sweet and good" (196), and she
dreams of the courage and sacrifices of pioneer women in
support of their husbands (200-201), even though what she
has to offer Paul is obscured from his vision by the "wall" of
her color (229). She speaks of "salving" and "replenishing"
Paul even as she resents playing the Christmas role of passing
the beer and pretzels to his men friends (244). Her day's work
as a maid expands her empathy for Paul in his daily humilia-
tions. Her protectiveness of her daughter Paulette's innocence
after the Santa Claus episode bespeaks an intense desire to
nurture (although an honest introduction to racism and
lessons on survival might be seen as even more life-fostering
for the little girl).

Giving birth to Paulette, of course, is treated as the most lit-
eral and emphatic example of Maud Martha's life-giving
power. This biological act makes her more conscious than
ever before of her personal power. Usually quiet and deferen-
tial, she barks commands to her husband: "DON'T YOU GO
OUT OF HERE AND LEAVE ME ALONE! Damn.
DAMN!" . . . . Don't you sneak out! Don't you sneak out!"
(234). She can finally assert herself against her mother:
"Listen. If you're going to make a fuss, go on out. I'm having
enough trouble without you making a fuss over everything"
(235). When the baby arrives sneezing, Maud Martha laughs.
Afterwards, she "preferred to think, now, about how well she
felt. Had she ever in her life felt so well?" (240). Her eupho-
ria, echoing Brooks's own experience of first childbirth (RPO

192), conveys a new sense of power:

> "Hello, Mrs. Barksdale!" she hailed. "Did
> you hear the news? I just had a baby, and I feel
> strong enough to go out and shovel coal! Having
> a baby is nothing, Mrs. Barksdale. Nothing at all."
>   . . . a bright delight had flooded through her
> upon first hearing that part of Maud Martha
> Brown Phillips expressing itself with a voice of
> its own. (240-241)

Given this experience, it is not surprising that the optimism
of the final chapter, based in nature, is clinched with the
announcement that Maud's second baby is on the way.

> George Kent and others have found this optim-
> ism problematic: The novel does run a danger
> course and is not without some problems. The
> intent is to persuade the reader that, despite
> what the novel refers to as grayness, life for
> Maud Martha is fundamentally promising.
> But the power in the images of frustration
> threatens to make any optimism seem willed
> and somewhat strained. (Kent 115)

Washington calls attention to the strong current of unresolved anger over racist and sexist slights, and Harry Shaw
finds that despite Maud's sense of surviving life power, resentment and anger continue (172). Christian comes close to suggesting a nuanced unity that transcends these tensions by
stressing the ordinary, "where racism is experienced in sharp
nibbles rather than screams and where making do is continu-
ally juxtaposed with small but significant dreams" (241).
Patricia and Vernon Lattin find that Maud "has learned to see

both sides [of life] without either being drowned in maudlin tears or consumed by anger," and they conclude that "Brooks suggests a positive way of life that can help one maintain one's self respect and creativity in the face of the racism and death which surround one" (142). They attribute Maud's balance to her early experience of love, a sense of place, and ritual. It is Melhem who perhaps comes closest to underscoring Maud's sense of life as a pervasive and unifying feature of the novel. She emphasizes, as does Maud herself, that a comic view of life embodies resilience, survival, and an acceptance of the mixed and often contradictory tone of experience, expressed, for example in the "comic, grotesque, and noble" mingled in the chapters on the grandmother's death and Maud's tumor. Maud's "ability to love," her sense of oneness with nature, and her "merging of affectionate, intellectual, and artistic impulses within an increasingly vital, moral synthesis" constitute her "existential values," leading to a "humanistic faith and its joy," "resilience," and "adaptive stamina" (93).

If we see Maud's sense of nature and her own life-giving power as central to her character, we can understand how she can contain seeming opposites and reconcile them through living, not through a rational philosophical solution. At various times Maud demonstrates an ability to hold opposites in suspended balance. Toward her family's favoritism for Helen, she can simultaneously feel understanding and resentment (177). Toward Paul she can feel a resigned loyalty but also sorrow over his colorism and the loss of family traditions (244-249). Certainly she can feel violent anger, out of jealousy against Maella ("I could . . . scratch her upsweep down. I could spit on her back. I could scream"-230) and out of righteous indignation at the department store Santa Claus ("yearned to jerk trimming scissors from purse and jab jab jab that evading eye" 317). But after considering a cat fight with the redhead, she checks her anger: "But if the root was sour what business did she have up there hacking at a leaf?" (230). A metaphor from nature expresses the marital problem to which she has increasingly accommodated herself and certainly is at this moment, when she is expecting her first child. And instead of striking or speaking out against the Santa Claus, she focuses on how to console her daughter and protect her from the ugliness of racism a little longer, a life-nourishing act. Although "[s]he could neither resolve nor dismiss. There were these scraps of baffled hate in her, hate with no eyes, no smile and-this she especially regretted, called her hungriest lack-not much voice" (318), the last note of the scene is her equally intense desire to keep "Santa every winter's lord" for her daughter.

Like anger, death in its drama, banality, dread, and posing of questions is vivid in Maud Martha's perception. Death becomes intellectually interesting and ultimately acceptable. She can see her grandmother as an "ordinary woman who had suddenly become a queen, for whom presently the most interesting door of them all would open" (155). She can imagine herself dead in the coffin, like Uncle Tim, and find the significance of life, at reckoning time, in small acts of kindness (167). By the last chapter, amid the glorious sunshine and the question of what to do "with all of this life," Maud imagines that "one could think even of death with a sharp exhilaration, feel that death was a part of life: that life was good and death would be good too" (320). This Rilkean sense of death as part of life prepares her to accept the shattering sight of the maimed veterans and gruesome reports of the latest lynchings with the confidence that

> the least and commonest flower . . . would . . .
> come up in the spring. . . . Come up, if
> necessary, among, between, or out of—beastly
> inconvenient!—the smashed corpses lying in

acceptance of death

strict composure, in that hush infallible and
sincere. And was not this something to be
thankful for? And, in the meantime, while
people did live they would be grand, would
be glorious and brave, would have nimble
hearts that would beat and beat. They would
even get up nonsense, through wars, through
divorce, through evictions and jiltings and taxes.
(321)

The darkly ironic tone of the "beastly inconvenient!" obstacle of corpses and the getting up of "nonsense" bespeaks an
Olympian distance and, finally, triumph. As Melhem suggests, "contemplating nature . . . reveals her own truth," and
"life-assertiveness" becomes Maud's conscious, chosen faith.
It is nature and a very personal sense of life-power that
funds Maud Martha's pragmatic optimism and resilience. It
both drives her righteous indignation over injustice and
checks her disruptive impulse toward outcry. It enables her to
"love moments" (220) but also frame the broad world view of
the ending and of Chapter 31, in which she responds to the
singing men on the street with a sense that comedy prevails
over tragedy:

On the whole, she felt, life was more comedy
than tragedy. Nearly everything that happened
had its comic element, not too well buried,
either. Sooner or later one could find something to laugh at in almost every situation.
That was what, in the last analysis, could keep
folks from going mad. (307)

The comic in literary tradition has emphasized not the great
principles people tragically die for but the dogged persistence

of survival in daily life among obstacles. It is allied to natural life processes, and it embraces pragmatic compromise. Maud Martha's ability to compromise, to hold in tension her ambivalent and contradictory impulses, gifts her with the strength to go on to the new adventures, including a trip to Africa, that Brooks later imagined for her in the proposed sequel. In the tragic view of high principle, such muddling through may seem ignoble, but in Brooks's and Maud's view, the daily struggle to "make a good Maud Martha" lends ordinary people honor: "while people did live they would be grand, would be glorious and brave, would have nimble hearts that would beat and beat" (321). The blood that pulses in those hearts is the force of nature in its myriad channels, encompassing humanity in its onrushing momentum.

Works Cited

Brooks, Gwendolyn. *Maud Martha*. 1953. *Blacks*. Chicago: The David Company, 1987. 141–322.

————. *Report from Part One*. Detroit: Broadside Press, 1972

Christian, Barbara. "Nuance and the Novella: A Study of Gwendolyn Brooks's *Maud Martha*." *A Life Distilled: Gwendolyn Brooks, Her Poetry and Fiction, ed.* Maria K. Mootry and Gary Smith. Urbana: University of Illinois Press, 1989. 239–253.

Hull, Gloria T., and Posey Gallagher. "Update on *Part One*: An Interview with Gwendolyn Brooks." CLA Journal 21.1 (1977–78): 19–40.

Kent, George. *A Life of Gwendolyn Brooks*. Lexington: University Press of Kentucky, 1990.

Lattin, Patricia H., and Vernon E. "Dual Vision in Gwendolyn Brooks's *Maud Martha*." On Gwendolyn Brooks: Reliant Contemplation. Ed. Stephen Caldwell Wright. Ann Arbor: University of Michigan Press, 1996. 136–145.

Melhem, D. H. Gwendolyn Brooks: *Poetry and the Heroic Voice*. Lexington: University Press of Kentucky, 1987.

Shands, Annette Oliver. "Gwendolyn Brooks as Novelist." *Black World* 22.8 (June 1973): 22–30.

Shaw, Harry B. *Gwendolyn Brooks.* Boston: Twayne Publishers, 1980.

Stavros, George. "An Interview with Gwendolyn Brooks." *Contemporary Literature 11* (1970): 1–20.

Washington, Mary Helen. "'Taming All That Anger Down': Rage and Silence in Gwendolyn Brooks' *Maud Martha*." *Massachusetts Review* 24 (1983): 453–466.

Five

The Rhetorical Power of
Gwendolyn Brooks' *Maud Martha*
B. J. Bolden

Gwendolyn Brooks' stature as the first Black writer to win a Pulitzer Prize, in 1950, for her second book of poetry, *Annie Allen* (1949), set the tone for critical analysis of her subsequent poetry collections. Thus, it is not surprising that her only novel, *Maud Martha* (1953), has been accorded only minor attention by literary critics. Part of the recent resurgence of interest in and analyses of the novel resulted, in part, from the feminist focus of Barbara Christian, in her essay, "Nuance and the Novella: A Study of Gwendolyn Brooks' *Maud Martha*" (1987) and Mary Helen Washington's essay, "'The Darkened Eye Restored:' Notes Toward a Literary History of Black Women" (1987). *Maud Martha* is Brooks' bildungsroman of a young Black urban woman who strives for maturity seemingly amid the most ordinary conditions: early childhood, adolescence, courtship, marriage, and childbirth, which bear an autobiographical resemblance to Brooks' own life.[1]

Part of the competitive environment for critical attention in the early 1950s might be attributed to the publication of novels by writers like Ralph Ellison and James Baldwin who earned international acclaim for their fictional works and recent rankings in highly publicized listings, such as the "The 100 Best English-Language Novels of the 20th Century" (1998).[2] Ralph Ellison's first novel was *Invisible Man* (1952), the story of a young Black man's struggle to manhood on a journey from the southern to the northern regions of America. James Baldwin's first novel was *Go Tell It on the Mountain*

(1953), a tale of an urban Black youth coming of age amid racial and family strife. Washington notes the numerous critical assessments accorded Ellison and how his "nameless hero was considered not only 'the embodiment of the Negro race' but "the conscience of all races," while reviewers denied Brooks' novel "any relationship between the protagonist's personal experiences and the historical experiences of her people" (443). Similarly, Christian contends that "Brooks' novel quietly went out of print while Baldwin's first publication was to become known as a major Afro-American novel" (240).

Brooks' exclusion from the showering of media attention bestowed upon Ellison and Baldwin may be attributed to a hierarchical positioning of literature featuring male, rather than female, protagonists or the limiting definitions imposed upon Brooks as a poet rather than a novelist. Yet, whatever the case, these early critical oversights of *Maud Martha* position contemporary critics on the threshold of uncovering, constructing, and revealing myriad critical interpretations of the novel that will enrich the canons of Black American and women's literature and criticism.

Contemporary critics are revisiting Brooks' *Maud Martha* to explicate the subtle nuances of the work and illuminate the intricacies of form, language, and theme for scholars and students alike. Ultimately, this will result in a redefining of *Maud Martha* as a novel of historic significance that predates the explicit feminist novels and critiques of the 1960s and 70s, yet it is one that features a young Black woman whose individual responses to marriage, racism, and economic oppression define the stagnant life of the Black community prior to the overt activism of the 1960s Civil Rights Movement.

One focal point of *Maud Martha* that invites closer investigation is the sheer rhetorical power that Brooks wields to tell the story of an ordinary human being. In her interview with Paul M. Angle, Brooks discusses how writers should use language, and notes: "Language should be used with care and precision" (141). In a later interview with George Stavros, Brooks comments upon her approach to words in the poetry collection Annie Allen (1949): "I was just very conscious of every word; I wanted every phrase to be beautiful, and yet to contribute sanely to the whole, to the whole effect" (159). Though Maud Martha is fiction, not poetry, it shares much of Brooks' affinity for economy of language, lyrical phrasing, and the effective rhetorical strategies that define her literary artistry.

Besides the fact that, primarily, Brooks is a poet, it is entirely conceivable that part of the poetic sensibility of Maud Martha stems from the overlapping constructions of the novel simultaneous with the poetry of Annie Allen. In 1944, Maud Martha was originally conceived as American Family Brown, a collection of 25 poems about a Black American family. Through many communications with her publishers and subsequent revisions between 1944 and 1953, Brooks reshaped Maud Martha into a novel of 34 vignettes, while still maintaining much of the lyrical and rhetorical quality of her poetry. Additionally, during this period of writing and revision, Brooks also wrote, published, and won the Pulitzer Prize for Annie Allen (May 1950). The rhetorical foreground of Maud Martha is one the most forceful elements of its structural format. This work easily fosters ongoing assessment of its unique poetic quality and resemblance to Jean Toomer's Cane (1923), which still defies a single structural or genre characterization. Using the tenets of classical rhetoric, Brooks argues for the humanity of an ordinary, Black, urban woman who matures prior to the Civil Rights and feminist movements in an environment of racial injustice, economic impoverishment, and gender and color discrimination. Historically, rhetoric has been defined as emanating from the art or discipline that deals with written or spoken discourse in order to persuade or move an audience to a pre-defined position. Early African and Greek scholars were well-versed in employing rhetoric to inform, argue, or persuade an audience or reader to adopt a particular position. In his text *Classical Rhetoric for the Modern Student* (1965), author Edward P. J. Corbett discusses early rhetoric and comments on "invention" as the first and most critical of the five parts of rhetorical discourse. Corbett explicates the three modes of persuasive arguments or appeals that rely upon the oral or written inventions in "artistic proofs": *logos,* the rational appeal; *pathos,* the emotional appeal; and *ethos,* the ethical appeal, versus "non-artistic proofs" which exist in laws, witnesses, contracts, tortures, and oaths (34).

In *Maud Martha*, critics often miss Brooks' persuasive discourse that creates a character whose firm grasp of the ethos, pathos, and logos of her own life empower her to defy the many obstacles that a non-caring, racist and sexist society places in the path of Black Americans striving for human dignity. In the unfolding narrative of *Maud Martha*'s suppressed rage, stemming from the racial and economic realities of her life, Brooks simultaneously defines the suppressed rage of the Black community. The restrictive cultural milieu is striking in the opening lines of *Maud Martha*. Logically (logos), it is not that Maud just happens to prefer the beauty of dandelions to alternate floral varieties; the reality is that dandelions are among the few flowers visible in Maud's poverty-stricken community. Maud expresses, then, a "make-do-ness" with her environment, as well as her self-image:

> What she liked was candy buttons, and books,
> and painted music (deep blue, or delicate silver)
> and the west sky, so altering, viewed from the
> steps of the back porch; and dandelions.
> She would have liked a lotus, or China asters

or the Japanese Iris, or meadow lilies-yes, she
would have liked meadow lilies, because the very
word meadow made her breathe more deeply,
and either fling her arms or want to fling her
arms, depending on who was by, rapturously
up to whatever was watching in the sky. But
dandelions were what she chiefly saw. Yellow
jewels for everyday, studding the patched green
dress of her back yard. She liked their demure
prettiness second to their everydayness; for in
that latter quality she thought she saw a picture
of herself, and it was comforting to find that
what was common could also be a flower. (1-2)

Brooks' command of rhetoric is evident as the seven-year
old Maud defines a world of beauty. The opening metaphorical language of the young Maud is diametrically opposed to
the stark language Brooks employs in later chapters like "the
self-solace," "millinery," and "at the Burns-Coopers'" where
the adult Maud, facing persistent instances of prejudice, discrimination, and racism, reconciles and represses her lyrical
language and adopts rhetorical strategies exhibiting the more
formal schemes of repetition to fit tense, racial incidents that
anger her. By contrast, the opening chapter is ripe with
metaphors of the "demure prettiness" of dandelions as "yellow
jewels" and Maud's back yard as a "patched green dress." Her
descriptions are enhanced by her use of rhetorical strategies,
especially repetition, as in "meadow lilies," "fling her arms,"
and the phrase, "to be cherished", that points not only to the
dandelions but to Maud's own sincere wish for a cherished
identity and existence.

So concerned is young Maud with the ethics and morality
(ethos) of her life, that she is certain that if only she can be
"good," she also will be "cherished." In "at the Regal," sixteen

year old Maud makes a lifelong decision regarding the ethics she will maintain in her life: a high moral character, self-esteem, and a proper image of herself. When she opposes the image of the star performer, Howie Joe Jones, and all people who "could parade themselves on a stage" and "exhibit their precious private identities . . . for a thousand eyes," she simultaneously defines her own identity. The passage ends with Maud's declaration: "What she wanted was to donate to the world a good Maud Martha. That was the offering, the bit of art, that could not come from any other. She would polish and hone that" (21-22).

In a later testimony to Maud's continuing resolve to live a virtuous life, she traps a mouse in her kitchenette apartment, then releases it. In "Maud Martha spares the mouse," Maud finally snares the evasive creature in a trap, after it has eluded her for weeks. But once she admits to feeling empowered by holding the life of another creature in the balance, she releases the mouse, rather than destroying it. Maud is elated:

> Suddenly she was conscious of a new cleanness
> in her. A wide air walked in her. A life had
> blundered its way into her power and it had
> been hers to preserve or destroy. She had not
> destroyed. In the center of that simple restraint
> was—creation. She had created a piece of life.
> It was wonderful.
> "Why," she thought, as her height doubled,
> "why, I'm good! I am *good*." (71)

Maud's propensity for maintaining a high moral character is coupled with her logical thinking as she realistically assesses her ability to garner a marriage proposal from the beau of her choice, Paul Phillips. In "low yellow," Maud understands that she does not epitomize the kind of beauty that would normally attract the color-struck Paul:

> I am . . . not what he can call pretty if he
> remains true to what his idea of pretty has
> always been. Pretty would be a little cream-
> colored thing with curly hair. Or at the very
> lowest pretty would be a little curly-haired
> thing the color of cocoa with a lot of milk in
> it. Whereas, I am the color of cocoa straight,
> if you can be even that "kind" to me. (53)

Yet, Maud's response to Paul's ambivalence over her plain-
ness and dark skin is to resort to her own ethical and moral
values, which she is sure will win him over: "But in the end I'll
hook him, even while he's wondering how this marriage will
cramp him or pinch at him, admirer of the gay life, spiffy
clothes, beautiful yellow girls, natural hair, smooth cars, jewels, night clubs, cocktail lounges, class" (55). Paul does marry
Maud, but he makes his color preference crystal clear in the
vignette "if you're light and have long hair," when he publicly
chooses to dance and flirt with the light-skinned,
"Goldspangles" Maella while Maud ruminates:

> But it's my color that makes him mad. I try
> to shut my eyes to that, but it's no good.
> What I am inside, what is really me, he likes
> okay. But he keeps looking at my color, which
> is like a wall. He has to jump over it in order
> to meet and touch what I've got for him. He
> has to jump away up high in order to see it.
> He gets awful tired of all that jumping. (87-88)

Although Maud initially adopts a "settling" attitude in her
marriage to Paul, stating, "'I'm making a baby for this man

and I mean to do it in peace'," eventually, she becomes more certain of her own identity and adopts a strident tone and reductive view of Paul's more pedestrian values (88). After struggling to elevate Paul's willingness to settle for value-priced furniture, life in a basement apartment, and a socially stigmatized, cheap "stove-heated flat", rather than steam, which came with apartments on the "better-looking street[s]", ultimately, Maud realizes that life with Paul will never be lived on the grand scale of her imaginary inner life (57). She sees and feels the cherished traditions of her pre-married life slip away, while "celebrating Christmas night by passing pretzels and beer" to a contented Paul and his friends (102).

Maud exhibits a decided predilection for the ethical and logical positions that define a high moral life and permit her to see Paul in realistic terms and to accept him as her husband, despite his limited acceptance of her. Yet, once she recognizes her own emerging identity, Maud represses her own feelings *(pathos)* about her place as a Black woman in a world that accords no honor or respect to people of color, and she demonstrates emotional staggering when confronted with clear instances of the racial discord and discrimination that Black Americans face.

For instance, in the chapter, "the self-solace," both Maud and the beautician, Sonia Johnson, hear the racial insult uttered by the white cosmetic saleswoman, yet neither responds to the comment: "I work like a n—— to make a few pennies. I few lousy pennies" (139). While Sonia brushes off her own lack of response with a "Why make enemies? Why go getting all hot and bothered all the time?" (142), Maud represses her anger in a different way. Unable to face a direct confrontation with reality, Maud pretends that the woman did not utter the unconscionable word, and considers a plausible response had she really heard such an epithet:

> If she had said it, I would feel all strained and
> tied up inside, and I would feel that it was my
> duty to help Mrs. Johnson get it settled, to help
> clear it up in some way. I'm too relaxed to fight
> today. Sometimes fighting is interesting. Today,
> it would have been just plain old ugly duty. (140)

Maud even represses an overt confrontation with Sonia Johnson: "Maud Martha stared steadily into Sonia Johnson's irises. She said nothing. She kept on staring into Sonia Johnson's irises" (142).

Similarly, in "millinery," Maud resists overt reaction to the condescension of the saleswoman who silently declares that she will not "cater to these n——— women who tried on every hat in her shop. . . ." Even with the price reduction, Maud silently exits the shop with the single comment, "I've decided against the hat" (155-6). Another instance of Maud's repression occurs following a single day as maid to a white woman who has instructed her to "always use the back entrance" (158). Maud is mute in the face of rude treatment, vowing never to return to the scene of yet another racial insult. Again, she has succeeded in repressing her emotions, stifling the legitimate anger that seemingly has no visible outlet.

Eventually, however, Maud grows from the disturbing realms of emotional turbulence to the solid ground of logical survival *(logos)*. From the seven-year-old Maud and wonder of dandelions, to the adult mother whose own child is confused by the indifference and rejection of the white Santa Claus, Maud refuses to yield to the societal pressures of racial, economic, and gender inequities. Instead, she redefines her world by what is pleasing to her own existence. As Maud enters mature terrain in "on Thirty-fourth Street," she makes her peace with life's discords.

On the whole, she felt, life was more comedy
than tragedy. Nearly everything that happened
had its comic element, not too well buried,
either. Sooner or later one could find something to laugh at in almost every situation.
That was what, in the last analysis, could keep
folks from going mad. The truth was, if you
got a good Tragedy out of a lifetime, one good,
ripping tragedy, thorough, unridiculous, bottom-
scraping, *not* the issue of human stupidity, you
were doing, she thought, very well, you were
doing well. (165)

In *Maud Martha*, Gwendolyn Brooks creates a character
whose surface simplicity belies the complicated structure of
the novel and of Maud's inner life. The ordinariness of *Maud
Martha* is intricately woven with complex rhetorical modes
that underscore Maud's ethical, emotional, and logical appeals
for understanding as she strives for human dignity. The novel
is replete with examples of lyrical language and the rhetorical
schemes of repetition. The early metaphorical imagery of
nature is central in "description of Maud Martha" ("dandelions"); personification of the audience as a single entity and
anaphora define Howie Joe Jones' presence in "at the Regal"
("The audience had applauded. Had stamped its strange,
hilarious foot. Had put its fingers in its mouth—whistled.
Had sped a shininess to its eyes" 20); and polyptoton introduces the "second beau" who yearns for an elevated intellectual life and identity ("Yet there are chaps on that campus—
young!—younger than I am..." 43), along with the visible use
of epistrophe and anaphora as David McKemster remembers
his mother who took in washing to rear her three boys ("Just
so they were clean, she had said. That was all that mattered,
she had said. She had said 'ain't.' She had said 'I ain't stud'n

you'" 44).

Finally, *Maud Martha* reaches its emotional and rhetorical peak in "a birth" when Brooks juxtaposes the well-paced movement of Maud's coming-of-age story with her height-ened emotional tension as Maud abruptly, but briefly, screams out all of the repressed emotions of her life. The impending birth of Maud's first child is announced in a phrase of asso-nance: "On her way back down the squeezing dark of the hall she felt—*something softly separate* in her" (writer's italics 89). But before long, Maud's agitation over Paul's role in her life gains greater clarity as Maud suspects that he is not up to the task of witnessing a birth. Brooks employs the repetition of anaphora to crystallize the point. When Paul attempts to call Maud's mother and the doctor, she screeches: "Don't you sneak out! Don't you *sneak* out!" (author's italics 92). And Paul's terror is vivid: "'Oh, my Lord!' he cried. 'It's coming! It's coming!'" (89). Finally, the repetition of polyptoton and anaphora illuminate Paul's reactions to Maud's screaming and the entire ordeal of birth: "He was glad of an excuse to escape. He was sick of hearing Maudie scream. He had had no idea that she could scream that kind of screaming. It was awful. How lucky he was that he had been born a man. How lucky he was that he had been born a man!" (94).

In the final segment of Maud Martha, it is clear that Maud has reached a plateau of individuality and a resolve to live life on self-defined terms. The novel ends, as it began, with nature imagery, suggesting closure in Martha's turbulent inner life. In "back from the wars," Maud's brother Harry returns safely home, and, once again, she experiences the beauty of nature and life, exclaiming, "What, what, am I to do with all of this life? (178). In her epiphany, Maud suddenly knows: "At a moment like this one could think even of death with a sharp exhilaration, feel that death was a part of life: that life was good and death would be good too" (178). After all of her appeals for understanding and acceptance, Maud Martha finally understands that self-acceptance is the first step towards defining human dignity: "She did not need information, or solace, or a guidebook, or a sermon—not in this sun!—not in this blue air!" (178). "The weather was bidding her bon voyage," (180) and she was ready to face a new season of life.

Notes

1. Gwendolyn Brooks, *Report from Part One* (Detroit: Broadside P, 1972). In the "Appendix," Brooks discusses the autobiographical features of Maud Martha, 190–193.

2. See "The 100 Best English-Language Novels of the 20th Century," published by the editorial board of the Modern Library, a division of Random House Publishing Co., 1998. Richard Wright is the third Black writer included in the listing, for his novel *Native Son* (New York: Harper & Brothers, 1940).

Works Cited

Angle, Paul M. *We Asked Gwendolyn Brooks.* 1967. *Rpt. in Report from Part One.* Detroit: Broadside Press, 1972. 131–146.

Brooks, Gwendolyn. *Annie Allen.* 1949. Rpt. in *Blacks.* Chicago: Third World Press, 1987. 77–140.

————. *Maud Martha.* 1953. Chicago: Third World Press, 1993.

Baldwin, James. *Go Tell It on the Mountain.* 1953. New York: Laurel, 1985.

Christian, Barbara. "Nuance and the Novella: A Study of Gwendolyn Brooks' *Maud Martha.*" *A Life Distilled: Gwendolyn Brooks, Her Poetry and Fiction.* Eds. Maria K. Mootry and Gary Smith. Urbana: University of Illinois Press, 1987. 239–253.

Corbett, Edward P. J. *Classical Rhetoric for the Modern Student.* New York: Oxford University Press, 1971.

Ellison, Ralph. *Invisible Man.* New York: Random House, 1952.

Stavros, George. "An Interview with Gwendolyn Brooks." *Report from Part One.* Detroit: Broadside Press, 1972. 147–166.

Toomer, Jean. *Cane.* 1923. New York: Liveright, 1975.

Washington, Mary Helen. "'The Darkened Eye Restored:'
  Notes Toward a Literary History of Black Women (1987)."
  Ed. *Invented Lives: Narratives of Black Women 1860–1960.*
  New York: 1987. *Rpt. in Within the Circle: An Anthology of
  African American Literary Criticism from the Harlem
  Renaissance to the Present.* Ed. Angelyn Mitchell. Durham:
  Duke University Press, 1994. 442–453.

Brooksian Poetic Elegance in *Maud Martha*

Dolores Kendrick

> *Rise bloody, maybe not too late*
> *For having first to civilize a space*
> *Wherein to play your violin with grace.*

—Gwendolyn Brooks
The Womanhood

Gwendolyn Brooks emerged through elegance in her own life. She was born into it, nourished by it, empowered through it: not that her family was wealthy or rich, but simply comfortable through the labors of her father. Yet the roots of her informed, classless heritage were born out of a family that resisted poverty, and dictated honor, courage, hope and self esteem-those characteristics we so often mistakenly assign only to the 'elite'. According to George Kent's biography of Gwendolyn Brooks, her "paternal grandfather, Lucas, a field slave, threw his master into a hollow stump and escaped to join the Union Army"(1). Such was her noble heritage; such were her family accommodations. If we are to understand elegance *as a refined grace or dignified propriety that expresses good breeding or good taste, (Webster)* then we can soon embrace the talent, origins and genius of Gwendolyn Brooks.

Though she was bred in poetry and music (her mother aspired to be a concert pianist) at an early age, in a sense her life was a poem, for it abounded in the syllogisms, life matters and raw epiphanies that often characterize poetry, and nurtured the exact visions to which she as a poet was heir. That being the case, she could hardly separate her life from her writing. In fact, in so many instances her writing depended upon her life experiences. Nowhere is that more evident than in *Maud Martha,* for as George Kent states: "Gwendolyn took an obvious pleasure in creating her pleasant neighborhood and family universe" (15). She also had an exceptional talent for, "twisting words into new applications of meaning."

> What she liked were candy buttons, and
> painted music (deep blue, or delicate silver) and
> the west sky, so altering, viewed from the steps
> of the back porch; and dandelions.
> She would have liked a lotus, or china asters,
> or Japanese Iris, or meadow lilies, because the
> word meadow made her breathe more deeply,
> and either fling her arms or want to fling her
> arms, depending on who was by, rapturously
> up to whatever was watching the sky. (143–144)

Thus Maud Martha's journey into herself and the world around her begins. Yet, it soon becomes evident that Gwendolyn Brooks, through Maud, is taking the Reader on a sustaining journey through the self, and in this exquisite passage astonishes and reveals the depths of elegance from which she, Gwendolyn, sprung.

In chapter two, "spring landscape: detail," Brooks describes children coming up the street in November:

> mixed in the wind, blew the children and
> Past the tiny lives the children blew.
> Cramp, inhibition, choke . . . (147)

(The last metaphor is reminiscent of Satin-Legs Smith, who wore, "ballooning pants that taper off to ends/ Scheduled to choke precisely. . . .") (43–44)

The notion of children blowing "mixed in the wind" suggests a natural revelation: carefree innocence amidst that which can choke or annihilate, and introduces us to Brooks' refined grace of language that accomplishes in a style that Kent suggests. We are introduced to a kind wind, not a destructive one that nourishes and enhances children, while "they did not trouble themselves about what cramps, inhibits and chokes." In simple but elegant phrases Brooks tells us that the children live in a decaying neighborhood, "the unhandsome gray . . . and little plots of dirt and scanty grass . . . " But their spirits are alive and floating in "bits of pink, of blue, white yellow, green, purple, brown, black, carried by jerky stems of brown or . . . brown-black . . . "(147). In other words they rise above the apparent dreariness. Yet, the elegant poetic magnitude here brings a language to root that surpasses that common phrase, *rise above it,* which when unattended diminishes into a cliché. Its not that Brooks disdains clichés. They have their place in living language. It's that in her genius she fetches the ordinary and emancipates it by counterpointing her language with a refined grace, a juxtaposition of seemingly conflicting ideas, so as not to belabor the point but to enhance it. A deadening cramp is an experience, as is to choke, but place these words in a description of a neighborhood, and the metaphor emerges bright and piercing with a restrained beauty and style. "These are lives in these buildings" (147). Brooks assures us. Yes, there is life here and the children announce it in autumn colors and their wind-blooming.

According to Kent, Brooks had a love affair with language through her earlier experiences with Shakespeare, Latin, Wordsworth, Keats, Shelley, and Byron. (These influences were later to be shared with powerful connections to John Killens, Dudley Randall, Inez Stark Boulton, Margaret Walker, and Haki Madhubuti.) According to Kent, it is significant that Gwendolyn believed that you could get the essence of a good novel in a short poem, that poetry concentrates language. (I have often described poetry to young people as concentrated orange juice.) This accounts for those daring excursions into language that not only reflect brevity, but also new tones, consummate images, and new awareness.

After a quarrel between her mother and father ceases, Maud Martha is "very happy . . . even though while the *loud hate* or *silent cold* was going on, Mama was so terribly sweet and good to her" (152). One can imagine the metaphors of *loud hate* and *silent cold* as perhaps written by a lesser writer: silent hate and loud cold. (The italics are mine.) Thus the language invention here, the Brooksian move from ordinary to the extraordinary by simply placing the wrong words in the right place.

The description of Maud Martha's living-room is singular.

> Three or four straight chairs that had long ago
> given up the ghost of whatever shallow dignity
> they may have had in the beginning and looked
> completely disgusted with themselves and with
> the Brown family. (158)

Basically, this personification is apt and regular. For here are chairs that have had a history, and in giving up the ghost reflect for a moment Maud Martha's loss, as she mourns her grandmother's death (whose funeral she has just visited). Yet, at the same time these chairs' "shallow dignity" reflect all that is superficial in the life of that house, while keeping intact its intrinsic worth. As Maud Martha, with a new eye, looks over her living room and as she focuses upon the "chairs disgusted with themselves and the Brown family," we suddenly realize that Brooks has taken us some place else: from the straight chairs into Maud Martha's world of herSelf, as she can no longer accept the room's former elegance in the state of mind in which she now resides. There is a restrained beauty of style here that at once describes an inanimate object so gracefully that it captures the inner spirit of the life to which it is connected: Maud Martha, who in her grief (for mourning has descended into grief), finds the "morning had become unspeakably vulgar, impossible" (158). But suddenly there is a pause, a jolt, an epiphany of sorts. Brooks brings a halt to the story-telling, and in typical Brooksian elegance she challenges us to make note, stop, observe, wonder, face the music:

> No matter how taut the terror, the fall proceeds
> to its dregs. . . . (159)

One must now look at the whole picture here; what is actually happening to Maud Martha in her inner life as a Black Woman. She opens the windows of the living-rooms as if in defiance of those racist innuendoes that "colored people's houses necessarily had a certain heavy, unpleasant smell"(159). And it is here that Brooks breaks the narrative and cautions us to listen. This kind of challenge can be seen also in *The Sundays of Satin-Legs Smith:*

> People are so in need, in need of help.
> People want so much that they do not know.
> (44)

In giving us this upon her boundless imagination, Brooks invites us again to a retrained beauty of style, a dignified propriety of good taste that inhabits and crystallizes her language to the delight of the Reader.

> What she wanted was to donate to the world
> a good Maud Martha. That was the offering

the bit of art which could not come from any
other. (164)

And again from *The Sundays of Satin-Legs Smith:*

He looks into his mirror, loves himself-
The neat curve here; the angularity
That is appropriate at just its place
The technique of a variegated grace.
Here is all his sculpture and his art
And all his architectural design. (44)

Note the Brooksian concept that delegates and redefines art
as a unique characteristic in the body Black.

She (Maud Martha) would polish and hone
that (164).

In contemplating leaving her home and the memories of
her family, Maud Martha touches the sentimental. But
Brooks changes the sentimentality of the moment to a dignified gracefulness:

But she felt that the little line of white, somewhat ridged with smoke purple, and all that
cream-short saffron, would never drift across
any western sky except that in back of this
house. The rain would drum with as sweet a
dullness nowhere but here. (172)

Maud Martha's strength of character that lends itself to a
total dependency upon what is natural, what is good, what
endures, what sustains, signals a bequest of survival at its most
dignified level.

Later we encounter the Brooksian elegant personification in tables that grieved audibly in Maud Martha's home. This particular description occurs in a situation where Maud Martha is grieving what she belies to be her inadequacy, her second-class citizenship, in a world she compares to that of her dainty, graceful sister.

Again, in describing David, Maud's "second beau." Brooks tells us as much about his character as his clothing in a single, elegant phrasing. David wears herringbone tweed, "(although old sensuousness, old emotional daring broke out at the top of his trousers, where there was a gathering that kicked back yearning toward pleat!)" (184).

In New York, Maud Martha's fascination with that city abounds as she envisions a world where "lustrous people glided over perfect floors" and whose voices "no matter how they rose, or even sharpened had fur at the base . . ." (192). The dignified gracefulness of voices with "fur at the base" so focuses our linguistic imagination here that it is not difficult to determine the societal level of the people described. (One is reminded of F. Scott Fitzgerald's description of the powerfully rich in Daisey, *Her voice is full of money.*)

The kitchenette building in which Maud Martha lives is the color of gray which manifests "the sibling, the frustrations, the small hates, the large and ugly hates, the little pushing-through love, the boredom that came to her behind those walls," (205-206) gray functioning as the basic metaphor here and used as a disturbing factor in Maud Martha's life. Even the "odors of fresh and stale lovemaking" are gray. "There was a whole lot of grayness here" (206).

Thus we come to a Brooksian definition of Gray, a color perpetrating a sense of doom or despair, or at least a sour caution. This re-defined word appears throughout the story, as if to suspend any doubt that Maud Martha is heir to a powerlessness to which she refuses to succumb.

A wide air walked in her.

In the chapter, *"brotherly love,"* Brooks compares a chicken to a human being, declaring that a chicken "was a sort of person, a respectable individual, with its own kind of dignity" with a capacity of "loving their children, finishing an evening meal, *arranging jealousy*" (295) (my italics). Later in describing Mrs. Burns-Cooper, who employs Maud Martha to do housework, Brooksian poetic elegance abounds in the word portrait of Mrs. Burns-Cooper: she possesses "an eloquent, angry bosom" (303), which among other known or unknown factors, dictates her character. Then, there is the chapter: *tree leaves leaving trees,* introducing a poetic elegance of its own, a language so taut, so dignified, so graceful that to call it metaphor belies its intent and startling beauty. Here Maud Martha takes Paulette to see a Santa Claus who is "unable to see either mother or child" (315). The incidence of racism reflected in Santa Claus' neglect of Paulette's Christmas wishlist, his lack of interest in the dreams of this black child (in a season of children) his indifference, even boredom, is thinly reflected in Brooks' language. When Maud Martha realizes that this Santa saves his good cheer and civility for white kids only, she simply says, "Come on Baby," and they move into a "wonderful snow" (316). As Paulette senses the presence of a hostile Santa, she comes to her own conclusion: Santa Claus didn't like her or look at her or shake her hand, to which Maud Martha offers Paulette plain and soothing answers of hope. It is here that Brooks' Maud Martha reaches a pinnacle of powerful thought that not only gives a purer definition of "good breeding," but also expresses the inherent good breeding of Maud Martha, herself. In the ethic of so many Black people of her time Maud Martha will not allow her child to become the victim of the obscenity of racism. She tells her daughter essentially that Santa's behavior isn't about her. It's about the costumed man himself. Thus Paulette learns to rise above it, and through her mother's eyes, to value herself. The chapter ends in a rush of stunning poetry that I have chosen to phrase in poetic form (which, of course it hardly needs):

> Keep her that land of blue!
> Keep her those fairies,
> with witches always killed at the end,
> and Santa every winter's lord,
> kind, sheer being who never perspires,
> who never does or says a foolish
> or ineffective thing,
> who never looks grotesque,
> who never has occasion
> to pull the chain and flush the toilet. (318)

Harry, her brother, is "back from the wars," And Maud Martha feels "the air crawling in at the half-inch crack . . . like a feather, and it tickled her throat, it teased her lashes . . ." (319–320).

There is sunshine in her room, and she is ready to renew, sustain her life, as she knows "wings (were) cutting away at the higher levels of air" (320). This is Her moment, Her Emancipation, if you will, another place of her continued epiphanies. So, she takes her daughter and moves outside into the sun and the blue air that for her holds joy and promises. Now, Brooks offers us the profound thesis of her story: Maud Martha as she stretches the Ordinary to the Supreme. She is Woman.

She is *Amira.*

Works Cited

Kent, George. A *Life of Gwendolyn Brooks.* Lexington: The University Press of Kentucky, 1990.

Brooks, Gwendolyn. "The Sundays of Satin Legs Smith." *Blacks.* Chicago: Third World Press, 1992. 42–47.

———. "The Womanhood." *Blacks.* Chicago: Third World Press, 1992. 113–140.

———. Maud Martha. 1953. *Blacks.* Chicago: Third World Press, 1992. 143–322.

Seven

Understanding Maud Martha through an Africana Womanist Conception: Notions of Self And Gender (Mis)Communications

Regina Jennings

The Pulitzer Prize winning poet Gwendolyn Brooks published her autobiographical novel *Maud Martha* in 1953, where she created a female protagonist who reflects africana womanism, ambiguity, and bipolar tendencies. Clenora Hudson-Weems' africana womanism theory provides a mode that globally explains the essence of African female thinking and behavior. It synthesizes why and how the African woman creates, responds to, and interacts within her environment. Because both Gwendolyn Brooks and Maud Martha are products of the racial linguistics of the postwar ethos, a pre1960s phenomenon, I will interchangeably use Negro, African-American, and Black as I investigate Maud Martha's actions. The issue of naming and being named in fact plays a key element in my analytical focus. Just as Richard Moore observes *The Name Negro Its Origins and Evil Use* (1992), I recognize that being named n/Negro significantly influenced how a people thought about and reacted to a pre1960s environment. Gwendolyn Brooks herself says that she found a phonetic discomfort in the word "Negro" although this is what she called herself prior to 1967 (Brooks, *Report From Part One* 83).

Hudson-Weems also considers the complexities and the erasures of being named or I should say accepting someone else's name. In *Africana Womanism* (1994), she separates and distinguishes her body of theory from feminist thought. Arguing that feminism is a useful body of theory for women

115

of European descent, she believes that placing "Black" before feminism simply appropriates someone else's language. And this once again positions African-Americans in another imitative instance. *Africana Womanism*, on the other hand, is a system derived from sole observation of African women, beginning an African/African-American historical point of entry.

This issue of name appropriation and acceptance figures in the double consciousness earlier theorized by W.E.B. Du Bois. Double consciousness carries the connotations of complete reliance on American experiences for self-identification. Maud Martha relies in part on the American dream of marriage, where the housewife is married to the home and the husband, not to financially assisting the family. This Victorian image is a springboard to how Maud Martha understands and charts her world. I see this when reading her actions as they inform her personal sense of self and family. In *Africana Womanism*, Hudson-Weems writes that: "the Africana woman is less inclined to focus primarily on herself and her career at the expense of the family and its needs" (60)—a definition and an interpretation that also suits Maud Martha, who becomes a wife/housewife and mother by choice. Yet, the ambiguity in her character addresses personality splits that attract the human need to look outward for meaning and affirmation.

Mary Helen Washington in her informative article "Rage and Silence in Maud Martha" says that the novel is about bitterness, rage, self-hatred, and silence that results from suppressed anger. Washington writes that Maud "expresses her silent and cold anger in manipulative and deceptive ways" (250). We see this manner of behavior particularly with her husband Paul whose innocence and playfulness sometimes chafe the protagonist. For example, after attending a "musicale," the newlyweds board a street-car where Paul entertains his wife, but she feels his "tricks" irrelevant and silly. She suppresses her dislike and what she believes to be a similar emotion of the passengers who watch Paul's playfulness "such as"

> cocking his head archly and winking at her, or
> digging her slyly in the ribs, or lifting her hand
> to his lips, blowing on it softly, or poking a
> finger under her chin and raising it awkwardly,
> or feeling her muscle, so that she could tell the
> difference . . . And because he felt that he was
> making her happy, she tried not to see the
> uncareful stares and smirks of the other pass-
> engers-uncareful and insultingly consolatory.
> (66)

Maud looks to (and away from) "the other passengers," believing that they commiserate with her annoyance. What I find interesting here is Maud's reaction and that of the genderless, ageless passengers to Paul's manner of sharing and showing affection. Maud's reaction contradicts her earlier poetic assertion about her "everydayness" and her "common" "ordinary allurements" (*MM 2*). Since childhood, Maud has wanted someone to adore and to cherish her; yet, this abstraction of romantic love diminishes, years later, in the reality of Paul. Also, because of her darker hue, Maud, has felt inferior to Paul since their courting days. Being annoyed with his public performance more than likely includes feelings of unworthiness and unwanted public display.

Maud Martha contains an important theme of racial aesthetics based upon the color stratification, exceedingly important to Negroes prior to the 1960s. During the 1960s, the traditional color schema for Negroes was challenged, modified, rearranged, and reversed. The reversal had to do with (re)shaping the image of the African, from the perpetual slave, hiding in the psychology of the Negroes.

Since African enslavement in America, the renamed slave/negro developed an appreciation of beauty and aesthetics that emerged from philosophers and statesmen. This negro[1] grew out of the head of Zeus[2] and is an emergence of Western myth and thought. European Americans elevated notions of beauty that portrayed racial divisions where the White was absolutely superior to the Black, not just in intelligence but in physicality as well. Reginald Horsman in *Race and Manifest Destiny* (1981) explores this truism by listing the many educated Europeans who articulated such separations. In *Race and Manifest Destiny*, Horsman traces how and when the argument for American expansionism included isolating Anglo-Saxons from every other race—deeming all others inferior. In America, God had chosen the elect, the colonies, to prosper; therefore, God sanctioned White supremacy, the slaughtering and enslaving of Natives and Africans. A variety of prosperous White men—lawyers, doctors, philosophers, and politicians—endorsed these ideas. And from this critical mass, the influential Frenchman Jean-Joseph Virey reached the conclusion during the nineteenth century that negroes were closely related to apes, not to other men (49). "Virey's work was praised and used in the American South in the 1830s" (49). In *Figures in Black* 1987, Henry Louis Gates examines such ideology adopted by philosophers and its affectation on the writing of Phyllis Wheatley. *Figures*, scrupulously hypothesizes the "white"ness of literary theory and its intertextual appropriation and modification for interpreting Black literature. Grappling with the conundrum of applying theory derived from racists to Black literature, Gates quotes leading thinkers of the early American period. By quoting David Hume, he argues how Immanuel Kant continued the following "prescriptive":

> I am apt to suspect the negroes and in general
> all the other species of men (for there are four
> or five different kinds) to be naturally inferior

to whites. There never was a civilized nation of
any other complexion than white, nor even any
individual eminent either in action or specula-
tion. No ingenious manufacturers amongst
them, no arts, no sciences . . . (18)

And of course Hegel believed that neither culture nor history existed in Africa. He credits any accomplishment in
Africa, specifically North Africa to Asiatics and Europeans.
Gates sums up this thought as a trope for African absence.
Paul Gilroy in *The Black Atlantic* (1999) argues that the
transatlantic African turned into a combination of what
Richard Powell in *Black Art of the 20th Century* (1997) cata-
logues as "American in origin, African in design, transatlantic
in praxis" (8). The "negro's" American origin is a multiple mix
of slavery, democracy, capitalism, conformity, distortion,
accomplishment, inferiority, horror, dislocation, and confu-
sion. The negro's American origin allowed the Whites to
decide and to fix a human antithesis. The negro was the anti-
human, the monster in the mind, according to the English celebrating Englishness (Gilroy 10)

Paul Gilroy maintains that culture is not specifically
African, American, Caribbean, or British, but all at once. Yet,
the tensions in the minds of White males when viewing a
"negro" certainly suggests extreme friction and harmonic dis-
sonance. If we follow closely how Maud Martha pictures herself, we can argue that the "negro" woman has absorbed the
"horror" of the White male's imagination.

This horror would explain why the African-American
female literary tradition begins with octoroon, extremely fair-
skinned protagonists. Fair skin is an emblem of beauty in *Iola
Leroy* (1892), and this emblem continues into the Harlem
Renaissance in *Passing* (1929) and in *Their Eyes Were Watching
God* (1937). Readers did not receive a major brown-skinned

protagonist until 1946, with Ann Petry's Lutie Johnson. Lutie Johnson in Petry's environmental determinist novel *The Street* is not biracial. She is objectified because of her beauty and poverty; however in color gradation, she prepares the way for the much different and darker, *Maud Martha,* the novella published seven years after. Both novels welcome a comparative analysis through aesthetics, economics, family, and autobiography.

By Maud's own admission, she is "common," fully Negro, and, for the most part, unashamed of her heritage. This dark-brown protagonist has a love of reading and the sensitivity of an artist, an artist of the self, not of a poem or a song. She comes from a two-parent home purchased by her father, the only provider for the family of a wife and three children. Maud's childhood, then, in no way resembles Lutie Johnson's. We meet Lutie full grown and beautiful struggling to find an apartment for herself and her young son. Her father had been an outlaw of sorts and her grandmother's advice did not connect with Lutie's imaginative yearnings. In contrast, the character Maud Martha had a wonderful upbringing, like Gwendolyn Brooks, herself. We travel with Maud in the novel through childhood, adolescence, marriage, and motherhood. Her childhood holidays, Christmas, Easter, Thanksgiving all had family customs and grace. During holidays, for example, Belva Brown, Maud's mother, would cheerfully decorate the home and bake special treats, making the familial atmosphere a snapshot of tradition. This is the family of Gwendolyn Brooks. Her father was a janitor and her mother a retired schoolteacher who invented a memorable hearth. Brooks recalls that:

> Home . . . always warmly awaited me.
> Welcoming, enveloping. Home meant a quick-
> walking, careful, Duty-Loving mother, who

> played the piano, made fudge, made cocoa and
> prune whip and apricot pie, drew tidy cows
> and trees and expert houses with chimneys and
> chimney smoke, who helped her children with
> arithmetic homework, and who sang in a high
> soprano: "Brighten the corner where you are!
> —Br-rrr-righten the corner where you are!—
> (Brooks, *Report from Part One* 39)

Maud Martha remembered similar moments that dissipated when she married Paul who could not afford a house, but a kitchenette apartment. Yet, Maud Martha was a housewife by choice following her mother. Lutie Johnson never had the luxury to choose. Economically disadvantaged, this single mother had to outthink and outwit wicked men who plotted her subjugation because of her delectable beauty.

In *The Street* and *Maud Martha* the theme of aesthetics and beauty has a central trajectory. Lutie Johnson is the controlling image of beauty. Maud Martha is the antithesis of loveliness, created by Anglo-Americans. Brooks takes two routes in terms of playing with pigmentation importance. For one, she values dark skin, because we empathize with Maud Martha who successfully catches a man despite her sister's advice. Helen, a charm among men young and old, warns Maud to abandon her love of literature in order to get a man, and Maud does want a man. Maud never imagines her life without a man, intuitively recognizing a male as a partner, provider, and protector. Hudson-Weems writes that: "The idea of the intertwined destiny of Africana men, women, and children is directly related to the notion of the dependency upon the male sector in the participation of the Africana womanist's struggle for herself and her family" (61). Maud desires a kind of development that male partnership allows. Secondly, Brooks frontally portrays the tensions inherent in the color stratification that emerges from Western racism, the horror that American Negroes (and those abroad) absorbed.

However, Maud's hidden response to her husband's playfulness on the streetcar reveals her ideas not so much about color, but of proper deportment. Maud's silent though seething behavior demonstrates the influence and the anxiety of conformity in the public sphere. During the post war period, the 1940s and 1950s, Negroes struggled simply to fit into society. Maud, uncomfortable with being on public display, never considers that the passengers may be envious because she has someone who loves her. Maud Martha desires distance from her personal needs and her world, enacting a unified version of courteous, quiet behavior, appropriate of a middle-class Negro.

With World War II over, America, the most powerful nation in the world, has a unified, Western version of culture that proliferates in texts and curricula. After the dropping of the atomic bomb, the reading public applauds literature that offers ironic humor, understatement, and indirection. Considered a symbolist writer, Ralph Ellison a master of indirection in *Invisible Man* (1952) develops a naïve unnamed narrator who presents palatable social criticism. This text sharply contrasts Richard Wright's earlier masterpiece of modern protest, *Native Son* (1940). Like *Native Son*, Ann Petry's naturalist novel has major and minor characters with flaws that tragically expand because of the environmental dynamism that portends destruction. In fact, Petry's naturalism recalls Wright's overt gothic environmentalism, and prior to him, Sarah Orne Jewett's clash of competitive values.

In the dominant culture, literature of the postwar period was largely based on the White male's search for self, for example, J. D. Salinger's *The Catcher and the Rye*, Saul Bellow's *The Adventures of Augie March*. In the fragmented narrative structure of *Maud Martha* written as an extended prose poem, we find this same search, as Mary Helen Washington writes, seeped in silences (249-250). Maud's silence on the streetcar and later in the bedroom does not permit Paul to grow into her idea of fulfillment. This pre1960s literary milieu offers Black authors the opportunity to revisit the crudity and cruelty of scientific and social racism, sexual repression, and their effect on heterosexual romantic love. Years later, this same decade of the 1940s captured the literary imagination of Toni Morrison who plotted several of her powerful and often poetic novels- *The Bluest Eye* (1970), *Sula* (1973), and *Jazz* (1992). In the following self portrayal, Maud reveals scientific and social racism that together ensure the diminution of the negro:

> I am certainly not what he would call pretty.
> Even with all this hair . . . even with whatever
> I have that puts a dimple in his heart, even
> with these nice ears, I am still, definitely, not
> what he can call pretty if he remains true to
> what his idea of pretty has been. Pretty would
> be a little cream-colored thing with curly hair.
> Or at the very lowest pretty would be a little
> curly-haired thing the color of cocoa with a lot
> of milk in it. Whereas, I am the color of cocoa
> straight, if you can be even that 'kind' to me.
> (52–53)

Both Maud and Paul reflect the aesthetics of White America and the leeching of the negro in thought, action, and reaction. Thinking her husband better because of his lighter skin, Maud adds the following to a conversation with Paul about having children. "I am not a pretty woman . . . If you married a pretty woman, you could be the father of pretty children. Envied by people" (54). Paul answers with,

> But I don't know . . . Because my features aren't

123

fine. They aren't regular. They're heavy. They're
real **Negro** features. I'm light, or at least I can
claim to be a sort of low-toned yellow, and my
hair has a teeny crimp. But even so I'm not
handsome. (54) (my emphasis)

The words, "fine," "light," "low-toned yellow," and "teeny
crimp" all portray the thinking, linguistics, and the aesthetics
of Negroes who grew out of Zeus's head. Paul's diction ele-
vates the ideal of Western aesthetics as it disparages features
that are "heavy," and "real Negro." In the above syntax, "but"
disclaims the previous acceptable and desirable features and
then drops them into the Negro abyss. This dialogue of Maud
and Paul is similar to and a deviation from Gwendolyn
Brooks' poem "The Life of Lincoln West" a genuine Negro.
In this poem, Little Lincoln's school-teacher, parents, class-
mates, and others dismiss him because of his color. Yet, the
little boy finds confidence in being called "the real thing," a
substitute for a genuine African. Paul Phillips separates his
African essentials from his Whiteness in order to isolate what
determines an upward social status.

After marrying Paul, Maud Martha decides that she wants
to fulfill being the best Maud Martha ever. This is the artistry
that she gives to the world—her world of Paul. Her dreams of
a luxurious apartment are dashed when his income demands
that they get a cheap kitchenette with a shared bathroom with
other tenants. The omniscient narrator introduces other tenants, children, couples, and particularly women and their care-
giving methods. In this montage, feminine mores surface.
This apartment house resembles a village where each family
has an idea of the quality of life lived within each apartment.
One woman never does laundry and rarely cooks for her husband; yet, her husband treasures her. This is a woman who
spends much time primping and painting. Another couple has

an open and closed love. Because they constantly spout love language to one another, visitors feel like intruders when they come to call. Another family buckles beneath the weight of many children and a dwindling paycheck, and both challenges cause the husband to leave. Then, a Lutie Johnson character succinctly and memorably appears. Her little boy calls out to her when she returns from work, "Here I am mother! Here I am! Here I am!" (116). His call dramatically demonstrates his need to be the most important male in her life.

In the everyday life of Maud Martha, we move from the general to the specific in instances of aesthetics and racism. In a beauty parlor, Maud Martha experiences racism indirectly as she reacts and does not react to hearing the word "nigger." A White saleswoman whom Maud thought so "pretty" and "pleasant" after selling Sonia Johnson, the proprietor, a set of unneeded lipsticks says: "I work like a nigger to make a few pennies. A few lousy pennies" (139). Maud decides that the woman had not "really" uttered the word to Sonia, another Black woman. Maud makes this decision based upon the White woman's appearance. "I'm glad though that she didn't say it. She's pretty and pleasant" (140). Maud further pretends that if she actually heard the word, how she might have responded if Miss Ingram, the White woman, had said it to her. She concludes that, "I wouldn't curse. I wouldn't holler . . . I would give her, not a return insult-directly, at any rate!- but information" (140). Both Maud and Sonia illustrate the powerlessness and the conformity of trying to fold into White society. The White woman invades the Negro space, and assumes and seizes control because Sonia Johnson defers to her with Maud complicit in the deference. After the intruder leaves, Johnson blames Negro people for being overly sensitive about language usage. Talking directly to Maud, Johnson justifies her silence by insisting that "nigger" is a form of behavior not an offense to Black people. Johnson continues:

Sure, I could have got all hot and bothered, and
told her to clear out of here, or cussed her
daddy, or something like that. But what would
be the point, when, like I say, that word 'nigger'
can mean one of them just as fast as one of us,
and in fact it don't mean us, and in fact we're
just too sensitive and all? What would be the
point? Why make enemies? Why go getting
all hot and bothered all the time? (142)
(my emphasis)

Johnson escapes the reality that she is already a benign
enemy of the White woman who assumes a social and cus-
tomary disrespect for Negroes pre1960. Johnson literally
dehistoricizes "nigger" by saying that "[it] can mean one of
them just as fast as one of us." To rectify her sensible cow-
ardice, Johnson creates a new history where "nigger" created
by racist enslavers represents both Whites and Blacks. In a
country where Negroes are relegated to the bottom of the
American spectrum, she simply and complicatedly seeks to
remain a business proprietor. She continues the desire of
escape by erasing herself (and Maud) from the category of
"nigger."

In popular culture, Chris Rock, the contemporary comedi-
an and host of "The Chris Rock Show" on HBO, does the
same in monologue. He mocks and separates "niggers" from
"Black people." Davarian Baldwin in his slammin' article
"Black Empires, White Desires: The Spatial Politics of Identity
in the Age of Hip Hop" reminds us that Arrested
Development also emphasizes this same departure—"niggas"
from Black people (146). This deviation for Arrested
Development seems rather ironic because this rap group projects an afrocentric thematic focus that celebrates racial soli-

darity. For Sonia Johnson, the gap sweats with sensitivity to language appropriation and this sensitivity in her view causes Negro and White tensions. For Johnson, to ease racial tension, she and Maud must simply dismiss reality, ignore racial insults, and, in the later words of Rodney King, attempt to get along. Silences, indirection, acceptance, suppression, and conformity are tools and criteria for Negro survival. This chapter closes with Maud Martha who "[keeps] on staring into Sonia Johnson's irises" (142), a bridge of denial and masquerade building between them.

The argument that Johnson presents to Maud is a prototype of the ideology postured by contemporary rap artists. Baldwin argues that "rather than evading the nigga, gangsta rap actually engaged and mimicked the position of nigga as other, as performance" (146). A White male student of mine who is a part of hip-hop culture in dress and music tastes, says that when he attended high school he was called "nigger." Baldwin quotes Robin Kelley who states that "nigga does not mean black as much as it means being a product of the post-industrial ghetto" (147). My White student was absolutely not a part of the ghetto, although Kelley refers to the new way in which Black rappers reclaim "nigga." According to him and Baldwin, the "nigga" is found in all segments of American life. To return to Martha, Johnson, and Ingram another curve emerges. Ingram does assume this language as a behavioral form and a negative one that she as a White woman disassociates from her sensibility and sense of self. Ingram is not a confidante or friend to Johnson yet she assumes in the utterance a familiarity that both Negro women permit. Nigga (nigger) may symbolize defiance-Black or otherwise—in postmodern America but in postwar society it remained the slave and the disgusting in the White imagination. Ingram reinvents herself through the use of nigger. She is better.

Other artists, spoken word poets, and playwrights continue

127

to juggle, revise, and transform the image and terminology of "nigger." The first American rappers, The Last Poets, during the Black Power era, reinvented and enriched the Black community and popular culture with the unforgettable rap/poem "Niggers Are Scared of Revolution," a precursor to Gil Scott Heron's "The Revolution Will Not be Televised". In the 1970s, Ntozake Shange's original choreopoem *For Colored Girls Who Have Considered Suicide When the Rainbow Is Enuf* made "niggahs" slip elegantly off the tongue. And today, Ice-T gives "nigger" machismo, using it broadly to illustrate when Whites make an outlaw power move on other people (Baldwin 148).

Nigger, it seems, as a synonym for Negro in *Maud Martha,* spotlights the variations that later writers and poets intensified and reified; however, the characters in the novel, Sonia Johnson, Maud Martha, and Paul Phillips often wish to escape being Negro. The contemporary rapper Mos Def has a track called "Mr. Nigga," where he showcases the patriarchal inner/outer disparity of being this conception—stopped often by the police and an object of derision. When rapping about the police he says: "They think that illegal's a synonym for Negro."[3]

Illegal is a synonym for Negro, along with other words that Richard Moore isolates for dismissal. In his important text, he argues for the immediate halt to references from enslavers, exposing the nefarious results that accompany parroting and parodying without historical insight. He writes that:

> [T]he emancipated people were identified by their color and branded by the names "negro," "negress," "nigger," and the like for discrimination, segregation, and social ostracism. Indeed, this campaign of caricature, ridicule, scorn, vilification, and debasement went even to the

lengths of exciting gruesome lynchings and
horrible massacres . . . Over 40,000 Afro-
American citizens were massacred during the
Reconstruction period in the South . . . As late
as 1905 the American Book and Bible House
. . . published A Negro A Beast . . . ***This name
"Negro" with all its vicious associations must
therefore be abolished.*** (Moore 48-49)

Maud Martha wishes to abolish and ignore the ugliness that
constructs the face of American society. She masquerades
attempting to make a quiet beauty around her. Jockeying
racial insults in the beauty parlor for her is an ugly business
that she tries to dissipate. Yet, she swims in contradiction
because in a previous chapter, she thinks Paul a coward for
shrinking from asking a White person a question. She shrinks
from such interaction and then blames her husband who manifests his discomfort publicly. Maud is similar to Sonia
Johnson in that she blames her husband (the Negro) for what
most scholars call the "Negro problem in America." In
Maud's imagination, Paul should be a White man, naturally
bold and adventurous. She characteristically omits that Paul
lives in his home country that has historically lynched or
humiliated men who exhibit such attributes. Being a Negro,
a synonym for nigger has stimulated American life and literature, with nigger now broadened to include Whites. Yet, I will
venture to say that in most situations for the Black, this word
still connotes the insult of enslavement and the hurt of inferiority.

In another direction, Maud Martha is neither erasing nor
attenuating reality. She harmonizes with it, when she brings
new life onto the planet. As Brooks in the first chapter creates
a child who trades places with flowers, when Maud becomes a
wife, Brooks has her identify with a mouse. With Maud in a

early on maud grows out of this

position of controlling life or death, she chooses life, saying this to the snared mouse:

> Go home to your children ...To your wife or
> husband. She opened the trap. The mouse
> vanished. Suddenly, she was conscious of a new
> cleanness in her. A wide air walked in her. A
> life had blundered its way into her power and
> it had been hers to preserve or destroy. She had
> not destroyed. In the center of that simple
> restraint was-creation. (70–71)

Subsequently, two chapters later, Maud Martha gives birth, and this birthing process stimulates africana womanist affirmations. Maud Martha gives birth at home without medication, with the help of other women: her mother and a neighbor, Mrs. Cray. In giving birth, Maud, in complete control, orders her environment. For the first time in the novel, for example, she tells Paul exactly what she thinks. Not only does she speak her mind, she shouts at him. When he starts for the doctor, she screams: "DON'T YOU GO OUT OF HERE AND LEAVE ME ALONE! Damn. DAMN!" (92). The epithet, "damn" at first in lower case letters, suggests Maud's newness in usage; however, the second shout demonstrates the power of labor. Paul is outside of this female picture. In "Perceptions of Men in the Early Works of Gwendolyn Brooks," Harry B. Shaw writes that Brooks is a portraitist of Black women and Black men (136). The portraiture of men, and in this case Paul, comes forward in understanding and empathy. Paul is a quiet hero "progressing and retrogressing in the various stages of the Black experience as he tries to cope with his environment" (136). In the novel, we learn of his aspirations for upward mobility, his work ethic, his love for his wife, his benign delight in a flashy woman, his friends.

Maud's observations make him quite human.

Through Maud Martha's interactions with Paul, we observe several of Hudson-Weems eighteen features of africana womanism. Maud Martha is "family centered"; "male compatible"; "respectful of elders"; "adaptable"; "mothering and nurturing"; and "strong" (143). Maud unquestionably demonstrates her strength as she gives birth. Without pretensions, she alarmingly and repeatedly screams and lies naked, covered only with a sheet. When her mother arrives, Maud demands "Listen, if you're going to make a fuss, go on out. I'm having enough trouble without you making a fuss over everything" (95). Maud had never spoken to her mother with such authority, and Belva Brown steps into her place as an elder, telling her daughter to "go on and scream. . . . You're supposed to scream. That's your privilege" (95). Maud's tremulous screams touched the genuine sisterhood that already existed in the apartment building. Mrs. Cray came to her rescue before Belva Brown arrived and she said to Paul: "I heard 'er yellin', and thought I'd better come in seein' as how you all is so confused." (93–94). Mrs. Barksdale came later. When Maud and Paul's daughter arrived, miraculously Maud shifts into another dimension of pure joy and pure strength. She thinks: "Had she ever in her life felt so well? She felt well enough to get up. She folded her arms triumphantly across her chest . . . " (98). Maud's apartment now welcomes other female tenants because nature will not permit the choice of total privacy. Hudson-Weems writes:

> There has always been bonding among
> Africana women. . . . In this community of
> women, all reach out in support of each other,
> demonstrating a tremendous sense of responsi-
> bility for each other by looking out for one
> another. They are joined emotionally, as they

embody empathic understanding of each other's
shared experiences. Everything is given out of
love, criticism included, and in the end, the
sharing of the common and individual experiences and ideas yields rewards. (65)

Mrs. Barksdale offered the light criticism with love when she
responded to Maud Martha's saying that "having a baby is
nothing, Mrs. Barksdale. Nothing at all" (98). Mrs. Barksdale
answers: "Well, from what I heard back there a while ago, did-
n't seem like it was nothing. Girl, I didn't know anybody *could*
scream that loud" (99). Maud, after giving birth, no longer
daydreams of her life with mother and father. She has her own
family now and the support of females nearby.

Maud Martha continues to grow into the idea of motherhood and male partnership. The novel does not end with the
daughter's arrival. In fact, the final chapters are clipped, open-
ended, and as with the entire novel, revealing. In one, Maud
interacts with her little girl, no longer a baby, in ways that
define other pressure points in American culture. Maud
attempts to explain to this intelligent child that an indifferent
and racist Santa Claus is something other than an unfriendly
personality and a representative of a broader rejecting reality.
Again, Maud represses the ugly and pretends something beautiful.

Yet, in Africana womanism, Maud Martha is a portrait and a
pattern of a postwar woman who desires completion and male
partnership along with children. Additionally, as a woman
(re)named negro, Maud Martha continues to suffer a series of
conditions created from the discomfort of growing from Zeus's
head. And as many, during and after this particular time period, Maud Martha adapts to surviving American racism with the
grace and the dignity of a Maya Angelou poem-she continues
to rise.

Notes

1. I am deliberately lowercasing the "n" in negro to reflect how early American authors, Black and White, presented the term. The degraded negro was not a person but an animal and a slave. In fact, during the early twentieth century, Marcus Garvey put together a campaign to force the press to capital-ize the "n" in negro. See Garvey, Amy Jacques, ed. *The Philosophy and Opinions of Marcus Garvey.* Dover, Mass: The Majority Press, 1986. Fairchild, Halford H. "Black Negro, or Afro-American? The Differences are Crucial!". *Journal of Black Studies.* Vol. 16. No 1 (1985): 47-55. Jennings, Regina. "From Nigger to Negro: Dysfunctional Beginnings in the Identity of Africans". *The Annals of African-Centered Psychology.* Forthcoming.

2. I have selected the Greek mythological God, Zeus as an originator of Westernism, a stronghold in Eurocentric studies For an interpretation of this prototype and its influence on White male thinking and behavior, see Tacey, David J. *Remaking Men: Jung, Spirituality and Social Change.* London: Routledge, 1997. The n/Negro is a western creation. Negroes did not exist in Africa and the indigenous Africans never referred to themselves as Negroes.

3. Mos Def *Black on Both Sides.* Los Angeles, CA: Rawkus Records, 1999.

Works Cited

Baldwin, Davarian L. "Black Empires, White Desires: The Spatial Politics of Identity in The Age of Hip Hop." *Renaissance Noire* Vol. 2 (1999): 138–159.

Brooks, Gwendolyn. *Maud Martha.* 1953. Chicago: Third World Press, 1993.

———. *Report from Part One.* Detroit: Broadside Press, 1972.

Gates, Henry Louis, Jr. *Figures in Black: Words, Signs, and the "Racial" Self.* New York: Oxford University Press, 1987.

Gilroy, Paul. *The Black Atlantic: Modernity and Double Consciousness.* Cambridge: Harvard University Press, 1993.

Horsman, Reginald. *Race and Manifest Destiny: The Origins of American Racial Anglo-Saxonism.* Cambridge: Harvard University Press, 1981.

Hudson-Weems, Clenora. *Africana Womanism: Reclaiming Ourselves.* Troy: Bedford Publishers, 1993.

Moore, Richard. *The Name Negro: Its Origin and Evil Use.* Baltimore: Black Classic Press, 1992.

Powell, Richard. J. *Black Art and Culture of the 20th Century.* New York: Thames and Hudson, 1997.

Shaw, Harry B. "Perceptions of Men in the Early Works of Gwendolyn Brooks." *Black American Poets Between Worlds 1940–1960.* Ed. R. Baxter Miller. The University of Tennessee Press, 1986.

Washington, Mary Helen. "Taming all that Anger Down: Rage and Silence in Gwendolyn Brooks' *Maud Martha.*" *Black Literature and Literary* Theory. Ed. Henry Louis Gates. New York: Methuen, 1984.

Eight

Black is Not Gray:
Maud Martha as an Argument
for Social Equality

Elaine Richardson

Gwendolyn Brooks' 1953 novel, *Maud Martha,* has, as one of its central discourses, the impregnation of the sign *gray* with a wealth of meanings, which signal her concern with the Black condition. In particular, her text explores Black assimilation to White cultural values that hinder Black aspirations. For Brooks, the melting pot metaphor of American racial, cultural, and ethnic blending does not describe the Black American struggle as aptly as the sign gray. In *Maud Martha, gray* signifies death, powerlessness, and ambiguity, as Black cultural values become filtered through White ones. In the remainder of this essay, I will examine Brooks' deployment of the gray motif as an argument for social equality.

Brooks presents Uncle Tim's life and death as gray. When Maud Martha is yet an adolescent, she attends his funeral. After observing his corpse, she notes that "It all came down to gray clay" (25). While reflecting on her memories of him, she tries to come to terms with the meaning of a Black life. She notes that "he had been easy with the aint's and sho-nuffs," (24) that he wasn't a heavy drinker, and that he exploited what "separate but equal" education he was able to attain to the best of his ability. For example, Uncle Tim "absorbed the headlines" of the *Chicago Tribune,* but he could not read the paper. He also "studied," not read, the cartoons in Collier's and the *Saturday Evening Post.* (24)

Uncle Tim's seeming inability to read deeply has important implications. Critical literacy theories hold that reading is an active process in which one brings cultural, political, class, linguistic, gender and other codes to a text in order to create and act on its meaning (Macedo 1994; Gee 1996). Brooks' description of Uncle Tim's absorbing rather than reading suggests that he is powerless to make meaning out of the newspapers or to act upon the discourses represented in the newspapers. There is no need for him to read between the (head)lines, or to read the paper from cover to cover, even if he can, literally, since the paper does not speak to the world as he knows it. He, rather, absorbs the headlines and studies the comics. What is written between the headlines for Uncle Tim is jibberish, ambiguous, or gray.

Another interpretation of Uncle Tim's seeming inability to read deeply raises the issue of unequal access to culturally empowering education. He had a separate but equal command of Standard American English and strove to read the newspapers as best he could. Unfortunately, it was an isolated striving disconnected from an organized cultural or political movement. Uncle Tim's education was neither culturally nor politically empowering, from either a Black or a White perspective. Therefore it, too, was gray.

In contemplating the importance of this Black life, Maud Martha wonders if the world had improved at all because of Tim. She considers the good deeds that Tim, perhaps, had accomplished and wonders what Tim would say if he had it to do all over (25-26). Brooks is offering a critique of that practice in African American religious cultures whereby people endure the wrongs of this world, doing good deeds, in order to have "Pie in the sky when they die."

Further describing the funeral, Brooks continues to contrast black and white imagery. A point of example is the scene in which the organist is playing a traditional Christian hymn "We Shall Understand It Better By and By" (26). This scene evokes Brooks' argument that one must reject the position

that change comes only in the afterlife. Maud comments that
the music, with its jazz roll, was gentle yet very suggestive.
Indeed, African American music is a defining element of the
African American vernacular tradition of struggle, "making a
way out of no way." Historically, enslaved Black people
adopted Christianity and its music infusing it with
Africanized ethos, making it fit into the material, cultural, and
spiritual realities of the New World. Black vernacular resistance and advancement practices must never be abandoned,
but adapted to new struggles. Therefore, the jazz roll in the
bass of the Christian hymn represents a scathing critique of
passive resistance, or should I say, passing resistance on the
part of Tim and others like him who have lost sight of the
empowering aspects of their Black inheritance.

Another example of Brooks' emphasis of White on Black is
offered through Aunt Nannie at the funeral. She is preoccupied with powdering her face, which is heavily covered in
white powder. The powdering of noses is a White bourgeois
custom that has been adopted by many Black people. Aunt
Nannie's face is composed. She is saving face, as she had yet
to shed a tear. The implication here is that Uncle Tim's life
and death are rather insignificant. Aunt Nannie's true face is
masked. Maud Martha wonders if this new widow should be
concerned with powdering her face! Not only is Aunt Nannie,
covered in White but so is the organist, who wore a white uni-
form, white hosiery, white shoes and plays a traditional
(White) Christian hymn (26). Thus, Brooks is arguing that
Black life must be defined on terms that are meaningful to the
advancement of Black people. In this way, the lives of Uncle
Tim, Aunt Nannie, and the organist are limited. It is difficult
for Maud Martha to determine the significance of Uncle Tim's
life and death and his wife's reaction to it. This leads Maud
Martha to conclude that she does not want her life's meaning
to be ambiguous, but heavily influenced by Black values.

Brooks makes this point in Maud Martha's reference to details of how she wants to be positioned in her casket:

> I want to be arranged in my casket; I don't want
> my head straight up like that; I want my head
> turned a little to the right, so my best profile
> will be showing; and I want my left hand resting
> on my breast, nicely; and I want my hair plain,
> not waved-I don't want to look like a gray clay
> doll. (25)

This passage suggests a heavy critique of the practices of inequality and cultural imperialism enforced on Black lives. Brooks' wording is careful and deliberate. She uses Uncle Tim's and Aunt Nannie's characters as symbolic of unorganized struggle. His head is "straight up" not "arranged." Her black face, covered with white powder is gray. From a Black perspective, one cannot fight cultural domination on the oppressor's terms. Thus, "straight up" is the improper way to go. One must instead come from underneath, with knowledge of one's full culture in a purposeful manner. Maud Martha wants her death to be associated with style, apparently a Black style—her head a little to the right, her hair plain, not waved. She wants to compose and show a natural self as her best profile (25). Expressing herself on her own terms will free her from gray self-destructive practices. The sentiment here is similar to that of Claude McKay's 1919 poem "If We Must Die," which was written during a time of racial unrest in Chicago and other major American cities.[1] This poem asserts that Black people must live and die in their own right. To wit, Brooks is arguing that Black men and women should fight,

[1] Henry Louis Gates and Nellie McKay. Norton *Anthology of African American Literature* (1997). See Note 1 page 984.

live, and die developing and defending themselves and their culture, rather than be hewn or fashioned into their places, as if clay, into (dead) gray dolls.

Maud Martha's experiences influence her developing consciousness as she moves from adolescence into womanhood. But consciousness of cultural oppression is not enough to save her from the experiences of adult urban life. After Maud Martha's marriage to Paul, they move into a kitchenette inside of the "great gray stone building" (60). The "great gray stone building" signifies America's solid social construction of Black lives. The move into the building is significant in at least two ways: confinement as a Black and confinement as a woman. As a young Black couple, Maud Martha and Paul are moving into another narrowly defined space created for them by society. Although Maud Martha's parents own a home and have a stable family life, society prescribes the cultural and economic foundation on which her parents and she and Paul can build. Unlike young middle-class White couples, who build careers, finances, and respect from their parents' names, Maud Martha and Paul inherit their parents' "separate but (un) equal" gray status. Like so many young people with backgrounds similar to theirs, the "great gray stone building" represents the foundation that has been built for them. A connotative meaning of gray is that it "[designates] a vague, intermediate area, as between morality and immorality" (*Webster's New World* 590). Spaces such as those represented by the great gray stone building often breed immorality. Like the housing projects so often rapped about in hip-hop lyrics, it is difficult to blossom in such an environment. Almost everything associated with the great gray stone building suggests death (Shaw 128) and contradicts life, liberty, and the pursuit of happiness.

In any case, Maud Martha is a very intelligent young woman. She loves reading. She strives to improve herself and to be a good, caring, concerned, and learned person. Yet, her future is as bright as it is dim or gray. Her move into the kitchenette building gives her a deep experience of life in the gray zone. The kitchenette residents are sentenced to a type of death in these tight quarters with roaches, mice, and bleakness. Brooks writes:

> [Maud Martha] was becoming aware of an oddness in color and sound and smell about her, the color and sound and smell of the kitchenette building. The color was gray, and the smell and sound had taken on a suggestion of the properties of color, and impressed one as gray, too. There was a whole lot of grayness here. (63-64)

Everything and everybody associated with the great gray stone kitchenette building become entrapped in everything that grayness represents: foulness, isolation, deferred dreams, death. The people came to embody the grayness no matter how bright or clean they were. The grayness represents internal conflict induced by external conditions.

Brooks' description of life in the kitchenette emphasizes the structurally induced strife on Black lives. This is not to say that greatness and the ghetto do not co-occur, for indeed, many great Black people have emerged from such conditions to achieve success by any societal standards. The life of Brooks herself is a case in point. Like the protagonist in her novel, she did not grow up in an affluent neighborhood. Although she was born in Kansas, she grew up on the South Side of Chicago. In spite of her surroundings, despite obstacles, Gwendolyn Brooks had loving parents and was encouraged and nurtured by them to become one of America's greatest poets. But in order to do this, Brooks had to struggle to become a self that only she and her family could envision, for the larger society was stacked against the average Black person.

The impact of White on Black is especially visible in the lives of Black women who must struggle to overcome unfair societal structures even within the Black community, since it has adopted many of the patriarchal and oppressive practices of the dominant American culture. From this perspective, Maud Martha's move into the great gray building symbolizes her even narrower, seemingly, less powerful place than that of the Black man. Maud Martha's relationship with her husband is also infused with gray. Brooks writes:

> [T]he little pushing-through love, the boredom,
> that came to her from behind those walls . . .
> via speech and scream and sigh-all of these
> were gray. [The] fresh or stale love-making,
> which rushed in thick fumes to your nostrils
> . . . these were gray. (63-64)

In "the Young Couple at Home," Maud Martha and Paul attend a musicale. Afterwards, she is expected by her husband to perform her wifely duties. Though she perhaps would have enjoyed making love to her husband, she longed for intellectual stimulation. Brooks positions Maud Martha on the bed reading the book, *Of Human Bondage,* albeit that she manages to avoid sex that night, while her husband reads, *Sex in the Married Life.* The reading of these books signifies that both characters appear to be trapped in (Black) American gender roles for men and women. Mary Helen Washington (1983) writes:

> All this muted rage, this determination to
> achieve housewifely eminence, this noble desire
> to be like the women of pioneer times-toiling
> interminably to sustain their men (the feminine
> mystique of the 1950s) masks so much of Maud's

real feelings that we are compelled to consider
what is missing in *Maud Martha*. (277)

Brooks depicts Maud Martha as coming into the knowledge of her own power, despite her position. Maud Martha's power lies in her ability to critically read her world for what it is and to try to intervene in it. For example, though Paul protested, she persuaded him into taking her to the World Playhouse, a White, well endowed, middleclass institution, that Blacks seldom visited. This scene evinces Maud Martha's desire for equal access to American institutions. According to Maud Martha, the experience made one feel good, as though one would return home to a nice "sweet-smelling apartment with flowers on gleaming tables" afterwards, rather than to the "kit'n't apt., . . . with narrow complaining stairs" (77). Paul enjoyed the experience, telling Maud Martha that they "oughta do this more often" (77). Her ability to fulfill her inner desires and have Paul to share in them demonstrates Maud Martha's agency.

But for all of her initiative, the role for Maud Martha is yet "downpressed" on the social hierarchy in both the dominant and subordinate cultures. American society's beauty standards require that the closer one's features are to the Caucasian, the more desirable one is. Because Maud Martha has a dark complexion and nappy hair, she refers to herself as "cocoa straight." Her intellectuality and her African features are slighted several times throughout the novel. For example, before she was married, her sister Helen tells her that if she doesn't stop reading, she won't get a boyfriend (39). Her sister Helen is the minion of her family and friends; but Maud Martha is just an old "Black gal," (34) as she is called by one of her sister's friends. Here again, Brooks shows that whenever Black values and ways of being are wholly devalued in favor of White standards, Black people, in this case, Black women,

don't think anything was said about Maud's confidence

suffer. Clearly, this situation is not separate and equal, but gray.

The lifeless properties of gray are even born into babies. When Paul sees his newborn baby for the first time, "[His child] appeared gray and greasy. Life was hard, he thought. What had he done to deserve a stillborn child? But there it was, lying dead"(97). From this passage, the reader assumes that the baby was stillborn. However, we know that it is a daughter and that it is not physically dead because Maud Martha heard the baby "expressing itself with a voice of its own" (99). But Paul's reflection on how hard life is for a Black child colors it "gray," "greasy," and "dead."

but this is Paul's interpretation not Maud's

The gray images (sights, sounds, smells, textures, spirits, lives) associated with Black cultural oppression connote, as we have seen, a plurality of meanings. These images not only suggest oppression and powerlessness in the lives of Black people, moreover, they represent sites of struggle. Brooks' exploration of these phenomena represents a vernacular discourse against which to read the dominant discourse. Brooks employs the sign "gray" indeed to show that Blacks and Whites were neither separate nor equal. The dominant culture's influence on the shaping of Black life is much too strong for that. On the other hand, Black struggle against oppressive practices has helped to shape America. That point is well made by Brooks' depiction of the struggling Black souls in her text. Out of sheer will to survive, Black women and men and their children are able to keep protesting, making a way out of no way, and critiquing oppressive practices. Perhaps this is why Brooks ends the novel with Maud Martha contemplating life and bringing another one into the world. Her brother has made it home from the wars and it is a bright sun shiny day:

[T]he sun was shining, some of the people
in the world had been left alive, and it was

doubtful whether the ridiculousness of man
would ever completely succeed in destroying
the world-or, in fact, the basic equanimity of
the least and commonest flower: for would
its kind not come up again in the spring? come
up, if necessary, among, between, or out of—
beastly inconvenient!—the smashed corpses
lying in strict composure, in that hush infallible
and sincere. . . . (179)
And, in the meantime, she was going to have
another baby. The weather was bidding her
bon voyage. (180)

The image of Maud Martha being rejuvenated by the sun is
very suggestive. It connotes a sense of health and life, that
Black people can be nurtured by getting in touch with nature
and themselves, that Black people must fight against the confines of oppressions, that Black people will always rise again as
a flower in the spring, no matter what.

maud's
realization
that greyness
will always be
there

Works Cited

Brooks, Gwendolyn. *Maud Martha.* 1953. Third World Press Chicago, 1993.

Gates, Henry Louis and Nellie McKay, eds. *The Norton Anthology of African American Literature.* New York: W. W. Norton.

Gee, James Paul. *Social Linguistics and Literacies: Ideology in Discourses.* Bristol, PA: Taylor &Francis, 1996.

Macedo, Donaldo. *Literacies of Power: What Americans Are Not Allowed to Know.* Boulder, CO: Westview Press, 1994.

McKay, Claude. "If We Must Die." 1919. *The Norton Anthology of African American Literature.* Eds. Henry Louis Gates and Nellie Y. McKay. New York: W. W. Norton, 1997. 984.

Shaw, Harry B. "Maud Martha." *On Gwendolyn Brooks Reliant Contemplation.* Ed. Stephen Caldwell Wright. Ann Arbor: University of Michigan Press, 1996. 124–135.

Washington, Mary Helen. "Plain, Black and Decently Wild: The Heroic Possibilities of Maud Martha." *The Voyage In: Fictions of Female Development.* Eds. Elizabeth Abel, Marianne Hirsch, & Elizabeth Langland. Hanover, NH: University Press of New England, 1983. 270–286.

"Gray." *Webster's New World College Dictionary.* New York: Macmillan General Reference, A Simon & Schuster Co., 1997.

Nine

Selfhood Revealed: Daughterhood, Motherhood and Silences in *Maud Martha*

Kelly Norman Ellis

*My belly swells with the moon of a daughter and
I dream of my girl life-Now or Later candy sticky
on my tongue, dirt on the bottoms of my bare feet
and reading Betty and Veronica comics under my
covers at night. My belly swells, and I remember
a self with plaits who loves to be melted in her
grandfathers kisses, a grandfather who smells of
Tuxedo Pomade. My belly ebbs under blankets
as I dream of my grandmother who makes soft,
milky grits in the mornings and sings to me the
soft nursery rhymes that never leave me...My girl
self...a true self...the still be self?*

Gwendolyn Brooks' first and only novel, *Maud Martha,* begins with a portrait of a young, "girl self": a place of impressionable consciousness where the world holds possibility and wholeness. In rendering Maud Martha's life in vignettes, Brooks documents poetically the slender shifting from girl to young woman to mother-woman. Most importantly, Maud Martha never looses her 'girl self', her whole, true self in these various transitions. She maintains the love of the simple, lovely elements of life: "candy buttons, and books, and painted music . . . and dandelions" (1). Although the roles of daughter, wife, and mother become part of her 'self', this true self remains firm and reaffirmed. But it is the role of mother and more precisely, the act of childbirth that allows Maud Martha to experience her own agency. Before that can occur however,

Brooks renders Maud's life as a daughter then wife. Her young 'daughter life' is one where her external voice is silenced, yet her internal one grows stronger. In other words, her true selfhood holds firm through the role of wife. Her third role as mother releases her from external silence and allows her to tap into her own power, verbal and nonverbal.

Introduced in Chapter Three, Maud Martha's relationship with her mother conveys tension. Her search for mother approval is manifested by her willingness to forgive her mother for the harsh "Shut up!" she hears after crying out in the night. Brooks writes: "The little girl did not mind being told so harshly to shut up when her mother wanted it quiet so that she and Daddy could love each other. . . . Even though while the loud hate or silent cold was going on, Mama was so terribly sweet and good to her" (10). This early chapter exemplifies Maud Martha's desire as a daughter. She calls to her mother to be comforted and is told to be silent. In "'Taming All That Anger Down': Rage and Silence in the Writing of Gwendolyn Brooks," Mary Helen Washington argues *Maud Martha's* style points directly to the protagonist's inability to speak. She writes, "The short declarative sentences, with few modifiers and little elaboration, are as stiff, unyielding, and tight-lipped as Maud Martha herself" (387). Washington points out that Maud Martha hardly ever speaks in the text, however it is also important to note that through the omniscient narrator, readers are privy to Maud Martha's desires and thoughts: her true self. Washington's critique focuses on Maud Martha's external language. What Washington calls "stiff" and "unyielding", Barbara Christian describes as an "internal conversation" filled with nuance. In the case of Maud Martha, the external language of the daughter is consistently silenced, but the internal conversation of her true self grows and portrays an intelligent, level-headed, observant and compassionate becoming-woman.

As Maud Martha matures, her 'daughter self' learns that her responses are less and less desired by others. The chapter entitled "home" exemplifies Maud's will to be heard. Ironically, the chapter also depicts her own awareness of rejection. After attempting to assert her own voice, "She knew, from the way they looked at her, that this had been a mistake"(30). While Mama, Maud Martha, and Helen wait to the hear the fate of the family home, Mama and Maud exchange words:

> "It might," allowed Mama, "be an act of God.
> God may just have reached down, and picked
> up the reins.
> "Yes," Maud Martha cracked in, "that's what
> you always say-that God knows best."
> Her mother looked at her quickly, decided the
> statement was not suspect, looked away. (31)

Clearly, Mama has a suspicion that Maud's remark is not innocent. But Maud's energy, her true self, sometimes beams through in her external voice. Even though Maud does not speak much in this novel, her voice and her intentions are frequently discerned. But, her honesty and energy are seen as unacceptable for a young, Black woman. Her intelligence and interest in books, as her sister states will "never get [her] a boy friend" (39). So this daughter learns to externally silence her true self.

This tension does not end with the mother-daughter relationship. Her father, in Maud Martha's estimation, prefers Helen to her. Her parents love her, but clearly, as Maud Martha's interior voice tells us, look more favorably upon Helen.

> Their father preferred Helen's hair to Maud
> Martha's . . . which impressed him, not with its

149

> length and body, but simply with its apparent
> untamableness; . . . Always he had worried
> about Helen's homework, Helen's health. (37)

But Maud maintains her strong internal voice which recognizes it is she, not Helen who:

> sympathized with him [her father] in his
> decision to remain, for the rest of his days, the
> simple janitor! when everyone else was urging
> him to get out, get prestige, make more money?
> Who was it who sympathized with him in the
> almost desperate love for this old house?" (37).

Clearly it is Maud Martha. She knows her contribution to the familial community, and her love of the family home is unyielding and without apology. Therefore, Washington's contention that Maud Martha does not speak much in the text is not exactly accurate, for it is the protagonist's internal voice that we hear, which is a truer, more honest voice.

My grandmother had six daughters. Beginning when she was nineteen, she continued to have babies until she was twenty-six. When I knew my grandmother, she was often silent. My grandfather's demands quieting her. He needed dinner on the table by six. He needed his insulin. He needed his shirts starched and pressed. He needed her. Before I was born, her six girls needed her. Plaits needed to be braided, noses wiped, tears kissed. My grandmother's silence was external, but she took to pen and paper and rebirthed her other voice, a voice that had lived within her always. She wrote plays and poems and short stories. She wrote down for her daughters and granddaughters, her own longings. After putting babies to bed, cleaning floors, cooking meals, she sat down at her kitchen table with her tea cup and talked to us with pen and paper although it would be after her death, after we found her words on pieces of paper that we would listen...

As Maud Martha moves into young womanhood, it is her role as wife that contributes to her external silence. Life with her husband, Paul leaves gaps and holes between them. The differences between the two reinforce Maud's outward silences. The silences and hushes of her 'daughter life' prepare her for a life as a wife. Her outward disappointment of her kitchenette home is replaced by a romantic notion. When told they will live in a stove heated flat, Maud voices her displeasure, "Oh, I wouldn't like that" she declares. But as the conversation continues she *"silently* decided she wouldn't" (emphasis mine) give in to Paul's desires. Then, internally, she reconsiders:

> Was her attitude unco-operative? Should she
> be wanting to sacrifice more, for the sake of her
> man? A procession of pioneer woman strode
> down her imagination; strong women, bold;
> praiseworthy faithful, stout-minded; with a
> stout light beating in the eyes. Women who
> would toil eminently, to improve the lot of
> their men. . . . She thought of herself, dying
> for her man. It was a beautiful thought. (59)

Maud Martha's internal voice which is typically strong and assertive becomes passive in this instance, for she has taken from her daughter life the notion of sacrifice and silence, and this silence momentarily spills into her internal voice. These external silences become larger during her married life: "They ate, drank, and read together. She read *Of Human Bondage.* He read *Sex in the Married Life.* They were silent"(68). But Maud's internal voice returns with the romantic stereotypes

erased. Once the roaches surface and, the flaws of her husband manifest, her true voice acknowledges these realities.
Ultimately, Maud Martha never loses her desire be "a good
Maud Martha," and when she realizes that she is "good" after
sparing a mouse, she voices it internally: "Why," she thought,
as her height doubled, "why, I'm good! I am *good*" (71).
Maud's desire to be good is not predicated on the opinions of
others, but on her own definitions of goodness. As the life of
a wife merges into the life of a mother, Maud Martha's internal and external voices become stronger.

*During my pregnancy I found myself drifting closer and closer
to my mother, but not just in the ways most women do. Of course
one talks of kicks felt in the middle of the night, the cravings for
jalapeno peppers and the nervousness of childbirth. But, I found
myself wandering through my mother's own swollen belly thirty-
six years before. As my mother sat on the edge of my bed and
timed my contractions, I realized we three (my mother, unborn
child and me) were now a new three: Grandmother, daughter,
mother. The shifting self is not just a shift in roles, for being a
mother is an unfolding of emotions, instincts and knowledge that
one sees through the eyes of the woman you have always been.*

Mary Helen Washington convincingly addresses the
empowerment that Maud Martha feels in the childbirth experience. Washington writes, "The pregnancy actually becomes
a form of rebellion against the dominance of both her mother
and her husband" (394). Maud screams at her mother,
"Listen. If you going to make a fuss, go on out. I'm having
enough trouble without you making a fuss over everything"
(95). And just as assertively her internal voice comments on
her mother's claim of "see how brave I was? The baby is born,
and I didn't get nervous or faint or anything. Didn't I tell
you?" To which Maud thinks, "Now isn't that nice. . . Here

I've had the baby, and she thinks I should praise her for having stood up there and looked on"(97). Maud Martha's mood
is one of satisfaction and pride. She is exhilarated by the
power of childbirth:

> Maud Martha's thoughts did not dwell long on
> the fact of the baby. There would be all her life
> long for that. She preferred to think, now, about
> how she felt. Had she ever in her life felt so well?
> She felt well enough to get up. She folded her
> arms triumphantly across her chest, as another
> young woman, her neighbor to the rear, came in.
> "Hello, Mrs. Barksdale!" she hailed.
> "Did you hear the news? I just had a baby, and
> I feel strong enough to go out and shovel coal!
> Having a baby is *nothing*, Mrs. Barksdale.
> Nothing at all." (98)

*The waves come stronger, and the nurse says I need drugs. She
wants me to be quiet. My moaning, she says, disrupts the routine,
upsets the women, frightens them. I am a good daughter, so I try
to be silent. I try and do the breathing my Lamaze teacher has
taught me, but it is not natural for me. I want to moan. I want
to groan..."Hold it down," the nurse says. She scolds me like she
is my mother. She is not my mother I remind myself. So I moan
as the wave comes. I groan from someplace deep. I groan cause
I know I am somebody's mama and that somebody wants me to
speak...speak up and out. I do not shut up. The nurse shuts the
door on my defiance. Next time I will scream I think. Not from
the pain, but from the power of my daughter's life surging forth.*

It is the experience of motherhood that moves Maud
Martha forward into agency. From the beginnings of the
novel, Maud recognizes the importance of mother love and
nurturing. When watching her grandmother die, Maud

Martha's first experience with death, she grieves for her grandmother's 'mother self': the only self Maud Martha recognizes
in her grandmother: "She who had taken the children of
Abraham Brown to the circus, and who had bought candy,
who had laughed-that Ernestine was dead"(15). When she
transitions from daughter to mother, Maud is allowed to
review her life as a child. She relishes tradition and believes in
life's rituals. The chapter entitled, "tradition and Maud
Martha," portrays the sense of power Maud would like to
claim as mother. Brooks writes:

> What she had wanted was solid. She had
> wanted shimmering form; warm, but hard as
> stone and as difficult to break. She had found
> —tradition. She had wanted to shape, for
> their use, for her, for his, for little Paulette's,
> a set of falterless customs. She had wanted stone:
> (102)

But she must be a wife too. Her role as wife becomes an
obstacle to her claiming her power as the mother she would
like to be. Her husband, Paul, rejects the beauty of tradition
and family and replaces it with his own desires. Maud Martha
remembers the traditions she was surrounded by as a girl and
longs for these "faulterless customs" for her own child. Maud
Martha maintains the true self of her girlhood, her pre-moth-
er life. Her internal voice speaking truthfully, and her external voice tinged with nuance, conveys what she really means.
Maud's anger toward her husband is externally silent, but
internally articulate and eloquent. The last image in the chapter, however, is Maud removing "from her waist the arm of
Chuno Jones, Paul's best friend"(107). This subtle gesture is
an act of defiance. This is the personality of Maud Martha,
her original nature. Her subversion of what is unjust or unfair

is done by the pushing away of a hand or the clearing of a throat. Martha breaks from her interior voice, however, when her daughter is present: a presence that makes it necessary to speak. After Maud gives birth to Paulette, " a bright delight had flooded through her upon first hearing that part of Maud Martha Brown Phillips expressing itself with a voice of its own" (99). This child is part of Maud Martha, yet has a voice that is uniquely hers: a voice Maud must teach her to use, and so, Maud Martha must speak.

In the chapter, "tree leaves leaving trees," Paulette is shy when talking to a white Santa Claus at Christmas. Maud encourages Paulette to voice her desires, and with some coaxing, her daughter opens wide and speaks, "Hello!" This moment in the text allows mother and daughter to speak side by side. As Santa ignores Paulette, Maud's response, "Mister, my little girl is talking to you" resounds (173). Although Santa finally acknowledges the two, he does so with disdain. This is a painful lesson for both mother and daughter. Of course, the daughter learns of white racism, but the mother learns that she must always speak against it for the sake of her own daughter's voice. In "the longest speech of the novel"(Washington 395), Maud addresses her daughter's disappointment at Santa's dismissal: "Listen, child. People don't have to kiss you to show they like you. Now you know Santa Claus liked you. What have I been telling you?" (175) The speech continues with Maud reassuring her daughter of something that is not true. Washington suggests that "the problem with her [Maud's] words is that they are still part of her subterfuge. She denies Santa Claus's rejection of Paulette and insists that Paulette deny her own perceptions of Santa's cold indifference" (398). Of course Maud does try to convince Paulette that her perceptions of Santa are incorrect, but she does so to keep from silencing her daughter in another way. To instill in her daughter a sense of power and wholeness by

encouraging her to speak is, for Maud Martha, an embracing
of her own agency. She tells Paulette, "You'll wake up
Christmas morning and find them [toys] and then you'll
know Santa Claus *loved* you too," (175) to affirm her daughter's sense of self and to develop that lovely, pure 'girl self': that
self which must be the core of every other role she will ever
play. Maud's rage at the white Santa for threatening Paulette's
selfhood is voiced, one again, internally:

> Helen, she thought, would not have twitched,
> back there. Would not have yearned to jerk
> trimming scissors from purse and jab jab jab
> that evading eye. Would have gathered her
> fires, patted them, rolled them out, and blown
> on them. Because it really would not have made
> much difference to Helen. Paul would have
> twitched awfully, might have cursed, but after
> the first tough cough-up of rage would forget,
> or put off studious perusal indefinitely. (175)

In the next paragraph however, Maud thinks of the "scraps
of hate in her . . . hate with no eyes, no smile and-this she
especially regretted, called her hungriest lack-not much voice"
(176). Maud's regret at not having voice is more a frustration
of not having the power to change the white world's responses to her child's blackness. Maud's early 'daughter life' has
shaped her silences, but as Washington writes, " . . . the most
important change is that Maud is given her most aggressive
role when she confronts the racism of that cool, elegant, white
fantasy world" (398). Maud knows that the world will destroy
her daughter's pure self by ignoring her voice, therefore
Paulette must develop a strong internal voice like that of her
mother's. Her internal voice will articulate *for the self and to
the self.* This is the "internal conversation" that Barbara

Christian so aptly names. One must know her true self, even if the rest of the world does not, will not acknowledge her.

My daughter has voice before she has words. Her first night on earth, she screams to me in her hunger. My tender, cracked nipples are useless to her even though I place them in her puckering mouth again and again. She sucks and screams and sucks and screams. I know she is hungry, and the nurses tell me to keep trying, but it is 2:00 in the morning, and she is still crying. I beg one nurse, the one who strokes my hair as I cry, to give her formula...please. She brings in an eyedropper and feeds my child. My daughter, Naomi, stops her crying and sleeps. Now, at nine months old, my daughter tells me what she wants as she learns words, one by one. I see her true self...she is curious and bright and loving and she laughs, she laughs, she laughs. And sometimes she cries. Not always and not often, but when she wants to be heard, she forces her voice upward, stirs the air around her, so I hear her, so I know her.

Of course, the novel ends with a pregnant Maud Martha embracing life with power and light, but what of Maud's own relationship with her mother, Belva? What of the silences and tensions between them? Between the silences there is acceptance and love as beautifully rendered in "Mother comes to call." The chapter does not ignore the normal mother-daughter tensions, but neither does it fall prey to sentimental images or clichés. Belva comments on her daughter's lack of cinnamon in the gingerbread and lack of a proper home, "A kitchenette of your own," (167) she adds. Maud Martha is a little defensive, like many daughters, under their mothers' critical eye. They discuss the status of her sister's life, drink tea, and gossip. Their mother-daughter conversation is typical with statements ignored and insecurities revealed. Belva says, "it's a hard cold world and a woman had better do all she can to

157

help herself get along as long as what she does is honest"
(168). Maud replies:

> It hasn't been a hard cold world for you,
> Mama. You've been very lucky. You've had a
> faithful, homecoming husband, who bought
> you a house, not the best house in town, but a
> house. You have, most of the time, plenty to
> eat, you have enough clothes so that you can
> always be clean. And you're strong as a horse.
> (169)

Maud's response is more a response to the disappointing
marital life she leads with her own husband. When old insecurities surface regarding her light skinned sister, Helen,
Maud is reassured by her mother. The delicately, nuanced
scene is layered with meaning as Maud externally voices her
feelings by saying, "It's funny how some people are just charm-
ing, just pretty, and others, born of the same parents, are just
not" (169). Belva replies, "You've always been wonderful,
dear." There is a silence between the two women that holds a
world, for they only "looked at each other" (169) with Belva
then praising her daughter's cocoa. They move from this pregnant moment to sharing the gossip that mothers and daughters do. They are comfortable with each other in their external silences and do not punish each other too harshly for the
little pangs and twinges uttered with words.

*During my pregnancy, I called my mother every day. Sharing
my terrified, joyful, confused heart with her allowed her the freedom to mother me: to mother me for the first time in years. I am
independent and thirty-five, but this baby scares me...My mother
listens in between the words...in between the "What am I going
to do?"s and the "Who will this baby become?"s. Mama coos and*

scolds. When this child arrives, Mama is there with hands extended to guide me over my daughter's new life. We talk every-day, as months go by. But some days are filled with too many "Have you washed her hair?" and too many " Does she have enough undershirts, a warm enough hat?" I become silent, con-vinced she is challenging my right to mother. She hears my silence and hushes. Then, she tells me that my sister has a new apartment, that Miss Ramsey has changed churches, that Rev. Thompson asked about me. I slowly speak again. Open up again to her words again. "Mama?...Huh? Whatever happened to that lady who went with Mr. James..." We move, comfortable in each other tongues. Forgiving each other in the silence.

Gwendolyn Brooks' novel moves gracefully through exter-nal silences to paint a portrait of one woman's journey from 'girl self' to 'woman self' to true self. This story exists in the spaces between the silences: the spaces between mother and daughter; girl and woman. As readers, we linger in the life of Maud Martha, peer into her secret spaces, watch her usher her daughter's voice forward, and we relish her fullness.

Works Cited

Brooks, Gwendolyn. *Maud Martha*. 1953. Chicago: Third World Press, 1993.

Christian, Barbara. "Nuance and the Novella: A Study of Gwendolyn Brooks's *Maud Martha.*" *Black Feminist Criticism: Perspectives on Black Women Writers.* New York: Pergamon Press, 1985.

Washington, Mary Helen. "'Taming All That Anger Down': Rage and Silence In the Writing of Gwendolyn Brooks."Invented Lives: Narratives of Black Women 1860–1960. New York: Anchor Press, 1987.

Ten

Maud Martha Brown: A Study in Emergence

Adele S. Newson-Horst

Gwendolyn Brooks' 1953 novel, *Maud Martha,* is an inter-rogation of color consciousness. From the beginning through the end, the ramifications of Maud's existence are tied to her appearance. The cultural context is Africana Womanist. *Maud Martha* is also a hibernation novel in the tradition that scholars associate with Ralph Ellison's *Invisible Man.* In the best Africana cosmological traditions, Maud Martha attends to a multiplicity of realities at once, thus, these three aspects of the novel work together to form a cohesive whole-one that speaks directly to the concerns and preoccupations of the masses of women of African descent.

Additionally, *Maud Martha* provides glimpses of the social conditions and political realities of the 1940s through the early 1950s. The life of the title character fills the reader with wonder-a sense of anticipation-as she moves through an inter-nal maze of responses to her reality. *Maud Martha* reflects a pivotal period in the social, political, and literary histories of African Americans and of America. Social conditions, politi-cal realities, and literary productions would evidence sweeping changes in the period following it. For African Americans, a new consciousness of self, within and outside of communities, would emerge. The life of the title character provides a road map of existing conditions and the anticipation of change.

Critical response to Gwendolyn Brooks' *Maud Martha* is as momentous as the period represented in the work.[1] After 47 years of being written about and situated into various tradi-tions, it is possible to view the work as a indicator of change in the literary and social consciousness of the academy. Initial reviews of the work were tepid, polite, and unsatisfying During the early 1970s, Don L. Lee and George Kent helped to advance a new reading of the poet (and the novel) as an emerging "conscious African poet" through their prefaces to her autobiographical statement, *Report from Part One* (1972). Later, during the late 1980s, feminist critics and scholars situated Maud Martha among feminist works. It is, in part, the excitement associated with definition that supports the endurance of the work.

In its interrogation of color consciousness, Gwendolyn Brooks' 1953 novel, *Maud Martha,* is thematically connected to Wallace Thurman's 1929 novel *The Blacker the Berry...A Novel of Negro Life.* Thurman's protagonist, Emma Lou Morgan, like Brooks' protagonist Maud Martha Brown, succumbs to the notion that "[t]he tragedy of her life was that she was too black" (*The Blacker the Berry* 5). In Brooks' metaphorical language, Maud Martha is, in spite of her character attribute, "poor, and Helen [her sister] was still the ranking queen, not only with the Emmanuels of the world, but even with their father-their mother-their brother. She did not blame the family. . . . They were enslaved, were fascinated, and they were not at all to blame" (35). The question remains: Who is Maud Martha and how does she elect to be in the world? The thematic continuum of color consciousness, Africana Womanism, and hibernation and invisibility interrelate in this novel to render a cohesive reading of her life emerging into greater consciousness.

As with *The Blacker the Berry,* the thematic and textual connections between Maud Martha and Toni Morrison's first novel, *The Bluest Eye* (1970), are just as arresting. For example, Pecola Breedlove and her family carry an emotionally crippling burden:

they believed they were ugly. . . . they had each

accepted it without question. The master had
said, 'You are ugly people.' They had looked
about themselves and saw nothing to contra-
dict the statement; saw, in fact, support for it
leaning at them from every billboard, every
movie, every glance. 'Yes,' they had said. 'You
are right.' And they took the ugliness in their
hands, threw it as a mantle over them, and went
about the world with it. (*The Bluest Eye* 38-39)

Unlike Pecola Breedlove who hides behind hers, Maud
Martha deals with her "poorness" with dignity and compassionate forgiveness towards those who buy into the ideal of
beauty.

These three novels, *The Blacker the Berry, Maud Martha,*
and *The Bluest Eye* address the cultural phenomenon of color
consciousness or the "intra-racial schisms caused by difference
in skin color" (*The Blacker the Berry* 38). This phenomenon
is a by-product of the race conscious drama inherent in
American society. The tradition of exposing this form of racial
violence extends back to the resistance narratives of the nineteenth century, during which ex-slaves provided portraits of
the house and field slave as well as mulatto and colored soci-
eties.

A menacing aspect of this phenomenon is the seeming gender advantage. In the novel *The Blacker the Berry,* Emma Lou
Morgan addresses it in her reflections:

she would show all of them that a dark skin
girl could go as far in life as a fair skin one, and
that she could have as much opportunity and as
much happiness. What did the color of one's
skin have to do with one's mentality or native
ability? Nothing whatsoever. If a black boy

could get along in the world, so could a black
girl . . . (39)

Emma Lou Morgan then moves through her life with prac-
ticed refinement, reminiscent of the "dignity" Maud Martha
practices very early in life. For example, at the white movie
theater with her husband, Paul, Maud Martha surmises:
"They looked at her hair. They liked to see a dark colored girl
with long, long hair. They were always slightly surprised, but
agreeably so, when they did. They supposed it was the hair
that had got her that yellowish, good-looking Negro man"
(76). Both *The Blacker the Berry* and *Maud Martha* suggest
that it is "easier" for dark complexioned men to make their
way in the world than it is for dark complexioned women. In
the end, though, it is Brooks' work which is least understood.
Her poetic approach to the issue of color consciousness coupled with the use of the novel as medium have long puzzled
those who rely on feminist critical readings of women's writings. Feminist criticism does not work here. A brief survey of
the criticism might help to elucidate this point.

In recent years, *Maud Martha* has been written about largely from a feminist perspective, though the debt owed to feminist critics cannot be understated. Mary Helen Washington
asserts that "without exception Afro-American women writers have been dismissed by Afro-American literary critics until
they were rediscovered and reevaluated by feminist critics"
("The Darkened Eye Restored" 34). Washington argues that
"Brooks's novel . . . though it perfectly expresses the race alienation of the 1950s, was totally eclipsed by Ellison's *Invisible
Man* and never considered a vital part of the Afro-American
canon" (35). She concludes that both Zora Neale Hurston
and Gwendolyn Brooks created narrative strategies that reflect
their concerns surrounding the empowerment of women.
Both writers:

enter fiction through a side door: Hurston was
a folklorist and anthropologist; Brooks is
primarily a poet. . . .[as outsiders] both were
freer to experiment with fictional forms, the
result being that they were able to choose forms
that resist female entrapment . . . (38)

Both writers prioritize race over gender concerns. This is an
African Womanist feature of their literary works, not a feminist feature. According to theorist Clenora Hudson-Weems,
Africana Womanism prioritizes race, class, and gender respec-
tively, which distinguishes it from a feminist/black femi-
nist/womanist theoretical construct (*Western Journal of Black
Studies* 187).

Enlarging on the idea of experimental forms, Barbara
Christian in her work, "Nuance and the Novella," argues that
the novel's fate of partial obscurity is largely a function of "its
poetic qualities, with the compressed ritualized style that is its
hallmark . . . and with the period when it was published"(128). She also says that Maud Martha "is not a tragic
figure, neither is she a domineering personality. . . . her
strength is a quiet one, rooted in a keen sensitivity that both
appreciates and critiques her family and culture" (131).
Clearly, this analysis alludes to several features of Africana
Womanism such as self-definition, family-centeredness, and
strength.

Similarly, Jacqueline Bobo maintains that *Maud Martha*
marks the first "depiction of an 'ordinary' rather than extraordinary black woman . . ." (*Black Women as Cultural Readers*
194). She goes on to say that:

It is thus a private tale with an interior, solitary,
and ruminative ambience. It is not a chron-

inner
consciousness

icle of a black person confronting a hostile white world but an exploration of the inner character of an individual. The effects of racism are implicit, rather than overt, throughout the work. (194)

Nonetheless, racism and race matter in *Maud Martha*.

In an interview Brooks confesses bafflement in response to one critic's "reporting" of the novel. Reportedly, the critic maintained that Maud Martha was not a hero. Implicit in Brooks' response is the idea of feminism's detrimental affect on the black community. Brooks aruges:

> But there are people who call themselves . . .
> Feminists and they mean something else by that
> word. In their cases it implies a corresponding
> hatred for men. . . . But I do feel that men are
> here in this world and that we have to deal with
> them. . . . I feel that is another divisive tactic
> and we Black women really have to look at it,
> look into the depths of that kind of advice,
> overt or implied. ("Honest Reporting" 26-27)

Brooks' response is indicative of an Africana Womanist perspective in that it displaces the primacy of gender and the struggle for power. Her response suggests the necessity of critical thought just as *Maud Martha* invites the same, for the novel is more than an answer to the question of what a woman can expect from life if she is not pretty. According to Euro-American standards, "Pretty would be a little cream-colored thing with curly hair. Or at the very lowest pretty would be a little curly-haired thing the color of cocoa with a lot of milk in it" (*Maud Martha* 53). Maud Martha offers a philosophy of coping, a way of living and being in the world under the circumstance of being as the narrator describes, "the color of cocoa straight" (53).

Hers is not a tragic existence, however. The tragedy would be found if she refuses to reconcile the contradictions in her life:

> She considered that word [Tragedy]. On the whole, she felt, life was more comedy than tragedy. Nearly everything that happened had its comic element, not too well buried, either. Sooner or later one could find something to laugh at in almost every situation. That was what, in the last analysis, could keep folks from going mad. The truth was, if you got a good Tragedy out of a lifetime, one good, ripping tragedy, thorough, unridiculous, bottom-scraping, *not* the issue of human stupidity, you were doing, she thought, very well, you were doing well. (165)

The practice of intra-racial strife and discrimination is a ridiculous tragedy, as it is born out of "human stupidity." I can locate no more heroic sentiments produced during the time period. Her realization that some black men have a phobia about dark-complexioned women does not ward off her desire for marriage, family, and a home. *Maud Martha* is a coming of age novel that takes the title character from childhood, during which she discovers early the idea of color consciousness, through adolescence, marriage, and motherhood. In the end, it promises a beginning, an ascendance from hibernation.

Because of the inherent philosophy of *Maud Martha* it is suggestive of an Africana Womanist work. Africana Womanism is a theory characterized by affirmation and engagement.

It posits family as a central concern and advocates that males and females work together to overcome the black woman's triple threat of racism, classism, and sexism. It affirms the black woman's reality by virtue of the fact that it is a theory descriptive of the preoccupation of the masses of people (particularly women) of African descent. Hudson-Weems advanced the term in the mid 1980s as a result of her observing Africana women, documenting their reality, and refining a paradigm relative to who they are, what they do, and what they believe in as a people ("Self-Naming and Self-Definition" 450). The theory is engaging in that it ultimately seeks to unite the Africana woman and man in the struggle for economic empowerment and survival.

Africana Womanism is distinct from feminism in its insistence on family centeredness and the prioritizing of the triple plight of Africana women. Feminism is gender-specific. Hudson-Weems discovered that, either consciously or unconsciously, Africana people are more likely to attend to reality in the order of race, class, and gender.[2] That is to say, Africana people recognize that they are appraised in social encounters first as "black," second as "poor," and third as "male/female." The politics of racial oppression is at the heart of the appraisal. While the vast majority of Americans would not lay claim to privilege based on whiteness, Africana peoples have a clear understanding of its machinations. Brooks' short story, "The Life of Lincoln West," first published in *Soon, One Morning* (1963) speaks to this phenomenon. While sitting in a downtown movie theater with his mother,

> a white man in the seat beside him whispered
> loudly to a companion, and pointed at little
> Linc. 'There! That's the kind I've been
> wanting to show you! One of the best examples
> of the species. Not like those diluted Negroes

you see so much on the streets these days, but
the real thing. Black, ugly and odd. You can
see the savagery. The blunt blankness. That is
the real thing.' (*Soon, One Morning* 318)

The story ends with his mother's pulling him abruptly from
the theater and Lincoln's elation at his "assessor's" designation
of him as "the real thing." The story closes with the explanation: "When he was hurt, too much stared at-too much left
alone-he thought about that. He told himself, 'After all, I'm
the real thing.' It comforted him . . . "(319). Little Linc is
comforted by the idea of authenticity-one of the eighteen
descriptors of Africana Womanism advanced by Hudson-
Weems.

The short story, "The Life of Lincoln West," was published
years after the publication of *Maud Martha,* yet the central
concern remains the same: color consciousness expressed in
both white society and black society. In the short story, the
protagonist is a seven-year-old boy victimized by society's ideal
of beauty. Like Maud Martha, the child is also "victimized"
by his family for "He would be sitting at the/family feasting
table, really/delighting in the displays of mashed potatoes/and
the rich golden/fat-crust of the ham . . . when he would look
up and find somebody feeling indignant about him"(317).
Victimization is a result of the unrelenting pressures of racism.
It is the result of living in a racist society. The human incli-
nation to compare, to distinguish, and to discriminate may be
done consciously as in the case of the theater incident in the
Maud Martha chapter entitled "we're the only colored people
here", or unconsciously as in the preceding passage from "The
Life of Lincoln West." The dynamics that ensue from the
color caste system, affecting whites and blacks alike, have a
catastrophic effect on personality formation. This recognition
is at the heart of *Maud Martha*. Moreover, because color con-

of a "color caste system"

sciousness is a by-product of racism, the novel is most suitable for an Africana Womanist critique.

According to Mary Helen Washington, the nature/distinguishing features of feminist literature of black women include: the recording of the thoughts, words, feelings, and deeds of black women; the success in heroic quests with the support of other women or men in their communities; the theme of women gathering together in a small room to share intimacies that can be trusted only to a kindred female spirit; the embracing of issues of social justice; the portraying of black female sexuality as a biological entrapment ("The Darkened Eye Restored" 35-37). Though there is evidence of Maud Martha's possessing feminist inclinations, she is not a feminist, emergent or otherwise. Of the features listed above, *Maud Martha* merely records the thoughts of an ordinary black woman. Hers is a partial retreat, for contemplation Hers is a partial retreat from adversities for the purpose of shaping a reality that would permit her, and black women like her, to negotiate a comfortable way of being in the world.

Of the eighteen descriptors advanced by Hudson-Weems, I will suggest how specific descriptors contribute to Maud Martha's way of being in the world. For example, Maud is a self-namer. In the opening chapter of the work, she is named and immediately defined through her amusements. Consider her reflections on the dandelion, a common, but unappreciated phenomena in life: "She liked their demure prettiness second to their everydayness; for in that latter quality she thought she saw a picture of herself, and it was comforting to find that what was common could also be a flower" (2). Maud locates herself in the scheme of the world with the metaphoric image of the dandelion. It is a matter of definition. For Africana women, Hudson-Weems explains that:

> Terminology is critical to definition, since
> words are loaded with meaning. Therefore,

when you name a particular thing, you are
simultaneously giving it meaning. The African
term for proper naming is nommo, a powerful
and empowering concept. In African
cosmology, nommo evokes existence, which
carries with it the total package. Since Africana
people have long been denied the authority of
defining self . . . it is important to seize control
over these determining factors now, lest we risk
eternal degradation, isolation, and annihila-
tion. ("Self-Naming and Self-Definition" 449)

When Maud asserts the idea that the dandelion is a flower, *dandelion yellow*
she invests worth in something that many regard as a common
weed.

As a self-definer, Maud resists the intra-racial discrimination and debilitating notions of beauty that she encounters
first at school and thereafter throughout life. She decides to
define the perimeters of her existence through dignity.
Though the reader may wish for a more aggressively angry
character, Maud Martha's calm responses to the indignities of
life are reminiscent of both the era of the 1950s and linked to
the tradition of Charles W. Chesnutt's work, *The Marrow of
Tradition* (1901), in which the central character emerges as the
archetype of the philosophical gentleman. Although Dr.
Miller, the central character, is a fair-complexioned and highly educated African American, he suffers the ravages of racism
in Delaware at the turn of the twentieth century. He understands the problem is not his but that of the whites in his community. He muses that "in order to live comfortably in the
United States, [a black person] must be either a philosopher
or a fool; and since he wished to be happy, and was not exactly a fool, he had cultivated philosophy" (59-60). Maud
Martha reflects a similar sentiment within the context of the

larger society and within the context of the familial relationship.

Central to Maud's existence is a concern for family-begin-
ning with her nuclear family and later with the family that she
acquires through marriage. Her empathetic support of her
father is as strong as her support of her "low-toned yellow"
husband, Paul. At the heart of her support, she offers them an
understanding of the politics of race. Yet, in a moment of
frustration, she questions the lack of loyalty her "poorness"
elicits from her brother and father. She muses, "Really-in spite
of everything she could not understand why Harry had to
hold open doors for Helen, and calmly let them slam in her
. . . face" (36). And similarly, in noting her father's preference
for Helen, she questions, "Yet who was it who sympathized
with him in his decision to remain, for the rest of his days, the
simple janitor!" (37). Likewise, Maud seeks compatibility
with her partner; though given the exogenous nature of the
larger society, one wonders at the ultimate success. She works
with her mate in the struggle to overcome the debilitating
effects of intra-racial discrimination in the community and
the ever-present discrimination in the society. In the chapter
"at the Burn's Cooper's" Maud understands for the first time,
"what Paul endured daily" in his work outside the house
(162). What Maud experiences for a single day as a maid,
Paul consistently endures as the bread-winner for the family.
This instance of discrimination in the work place, quietly
speaks to the reality of a shared struggle.

Maud Martha is grounded in the realities of her cultural
heritage. She is indeed authentic. In addition to images laced
throughout the work—from the stirring images "of sweet
potato pie that would be served at home" (5) and the strange-
ness of the people that she saw East of Cottage Grove, the
chapter "second beau" reveals her depth of cultural grounding
and her disdain for an inauthentic existence. Maud's descrip-

tion of her second boyfriend opens: "and-don't laugh-he wanted a dog. A picture of the English country gentleman. Roaming the rustic hill. He had not yet bought a pipe. He would immediately" (42). Her reflections on him are presented as dispassionate observations-without anger or regret. Her tone is suggestive of pity. The beau both rejects and exhibits anger over his humble beginnings: "what chance was there for anybody coming out of a set of conditions that never allowed for the prevalence of sensitive, and intellectual, yet almost frivolous, dinner-table discussions of Parrington across four-year-old heads?"(44). David McKemster compares his life and the life of his white counterparts at the university. That he imagines the superior intelligence of whites, speaks to his lack of cultural grounding. McKemster, then, serves as a foil for the authentic and flexible character of Maud Martha.

As a flexible role player, Maud manuevers easily from one role to another. She is, at once, a dutiful daughter, a companionable wife, and a loving mother. By the end of the novel, there is a sense of her coming into being an individual, without the threat of compromise to her other roles. She has just that much life within her. It is a life that has consistently reflected respect for elders and ancestors. In comparing herself with her sister Helen, she muses, "I'm much smarter. I read books and newspapers and old folks like to talk with me . . ." (35). The chapter "death of Grandmother" provides insight into the extent of awe Maud has for both her elders and death. What is clear by the end of the chapter is the way in which she fashions her memories, and the status and understanding that she gives her grandmother. She creates a space for her that is not connected with the reality of her dying. She chooses not to remember her grandmother in her near-death state: "Elongated, pulpy-looking face. Closed eyes; lashes damp-appearing, heavy lids. Straight flat thin form. . . . the voice thick and raw" (12), but rather, Maud chooses to reflect upon her grandmother's life: "She who had taken the children of Abraham Brown to the circus, and who had bought them pink popcorn, and Peanut crinkle candy, who had laughed-that Ernestine was dead" (15).

In addition to the above descriptors which are central to Maud's way of being in the world, the situation of the story centers on the desire for male/female compatibility in the face of the triple threat of racism, classism, and sexism. Hudson-Weems argues that it is not possible to take the theoretical framework of feminism and make it fit the particular circumstances of Africana women. Neither feminism's inception nor its agenda accommodates the Africana woman.

One of the many themes artfully woven into this 1953 novel is an ascendance from hibernation. Consider that the country itself had only recently emerged from the sleep of the Great Depression. Similarly, in the social, political, and legal spheres, the awakening that would lead to the Civil Rights era began. Recall that the unnamed protagonist of *Invisible Man* (1952) "is in a state of hibernation" (5). His hibernation is a result of his realization of his social invisibility. He adds "when you have lived invisible as long as I have you develop a certain ingenuity" (6). In the prologue the protagonist defines hibernation as "a covert preparation for a more overt action" (11). This metaphor alludes to the internal musings, interrogations, and investigations of Maud Martha. Implicated in this state of hibernation is a retreat from adversity; a resting period.

Similarly, Mary Helen Washington asserts that *Maud Martha* perfectly expresses the race alienation during the period of the 1950s ("The Darkened Eye Restored" 35). Unwittingly she compares *Maud Martha* and *Invisible Man*. Though she maintains that "there are no women in this tradition hibernating in dark holes contemplating their invisibility" (35), I contend that this is precisely what Maud Martha does. She is in a state of hibernation. Her dark hole is the kitchenette to which she is fated after marriage to Paul. It is a small, two-room, third-floor apartment with no bathroom, located in a great grey building:

> And these things-roaches, and having to be
> satisfied with the place as it was-were not the
> only annoyances that had to be reckoned with.
> She was becoming aware of an an oddness in
> color and sound and smell about her, the color
> and sound and smell of the kitchenette building.
> The color was gray, and the smell and sound
> had taken on a suggestion of the properties of
> color, and impressed one as gray, too. (63)

It is from this dismal place (which is reminiscent of the underground residence of the Invisible Man) that she tells the greater portion of her story. Her previous objection to moving into a basement apartment are quelled, by her reflections: "Was her attitude unco-operative? Should she be wanting to sacrifice more, for the sake of her man? A procession of pioneer women strode down her imagination . . . She thought of herself, dying for her man. It was a beautiful thought" (58-59). Like the sentiments in the speech that earn the Invisible Man the calfskin brief case, hers is a belief in the rightness of things, the belief in the institution of marriage as a safe haven and in her abilities as a woman to support her man. Over time she learns that her husband is unable to see beyond her complexion and that he too is overwhelmed by the reality of American racism.

Maud Martha's invisibility is demonstrated repeatedly throughout the novel. Recall the incident from her childhood when Emmanuel approaches Maud and her sister in his wagon as they walk home from school:

> "How about a ride?" Emmanuel had hailed.
> She had, daringly-it was not her way, not her
> native way-made a quip. A "sophisticated"
> quip. "Hi, handsome!" Instantly he had
> scowled, his dark face darkening. "I don't
> mean you, you old black gal," little Emmanuel
> had exclaimed. "I mean Helen." (33-34)

In *Report from Part One,* Brooks reports that the incident is factual —"The little character Emmanuel there, however, was real, even unto the name. How I hated my own Emmanuel! (It may be remembered that Emmanuel's phobia was dark-complexioned girls.)" (191). Brooks admits to enjoying a delight of her skin color before her entry into the school system. But, she explains, "As for Men in the world of School-the little Bright ones *looked through me* if I happened to inconvenience their vision, and those of my hue rechristened me Ol' Black Gal" (emphasis mine 38).

This very real experience of invisibility is extended beyond the community to the larger society. Her short-lived experience as maid at the Burns-Cooper's home as well as her experience in "millinery" speak to her invisibility. That the junior and senior Burns-Cooper could look at her "As his boss looked at Paul, [her husband] so these people looked at her. As though she were a child, a ridiculous one, and one that ought to be given a little shaking . . ." (162), and that the sales manager could insist that she is a regular customer in spite of her quite assertion, "I've never been in the store before" (156), speak to her invisibility. In these cases, the lives of Negroes are pre-determined by whites without the benefit of collaboration. The anger characteristic of *The Blacker the Berry* and *The Bluest Eye* are largely absent or muted in Brooks' work. Apart from differences in character, the muted anger is class and era driven. The Browns are near middle class and the decades of the 1940s and 1950s might well be characterized as a time of feminine restraint and refinement for middle class Negroes.

Furthermore, the last line of the book is key to an emergence from hibernation: "The weather was bidding her bon voyage" (180). Brooks explains in *Report from Part One* that "the first passage I wrote of this novel I did not use until I reached the opening of the last chapter" (193). If indeed the last was conceived of as the first, the book accounts for Maud's activities in hibernation. She contemplates her individual self situated in the socio-political domestic realties of her day. Her concern with "aesthetics" and/or color intimidation is ongoing. Maud Martha does not buy into the Euro-American standard of beauty, rather she interrogates it and offers a philosophy of understanding through Africana Womanist thought that would enable her to be in the world.

Gwendolyn Brooks' lone novel, *Maud Martha,* has much to offer the African American Literary Tradition. At the heart of the literature is a critique of America, and by extension, a critique of identity formation. The tradition may be viewed as one long and connected quest for identity and attendant ways of being in the world. Brooks' Maud Martha is the archetype of the emerging Africana woman. Her identity emerges from the historical reality of the time, from literary experimentation, and from a sub-tradition that treats color consciousness.

Notes

1. The novel, published three years after Brooks received the Pulitzer Prize for her poetry volume *Annie Allen,* was originally conceived of as a series of 25 poems about an American Negro family with the working title "American Family Brown" (Melhem 80).

2. There may be some variation in the case of Africana males who have been popularly demonized as "criminals."

Works Cited

Anonymous. "Briefly Noted Fiction." *The New Yorker.* 29 (October 10, 1953): 153.

Bobo, Jacqueline. *Black Women as Cultural Readers.* New York: Columbia University Press, 1998. 193–195.

Brooks, Gwendolyn. "The Life of Lincoln West." *In Soon, One Morning: New Writing by American Negroes, 1940–1962.* Ed. Herbert Hill. New York: Alfred A. Knopf, 1963. 316-319.

———. *Maud Martha.* 1953. Chicago: Third World Press, 1993.

———. *Report from Part One.* Detroit: Broadside Press, 1972.

Chesnutt, Charles. *The Marrow of Tradition.* 1901. Ann Arbor: The University of Michigan Press, 1969.

Creekmore, Hubert. "Daydreams in Flight." *New York Times Book Review.* (October 4, 1953): 4.

Christian, Barbara. "Nuance and the Novella: A Study of Gwendolyn Brooks's *Maud Martha.*" *In Black Feminist Criticism.* New York: Pergamon Press, 1985. 127–141.

Hill, Herbert. *Soon, One Morning: New Writings by American Negroes 1940–1962.* New York: Alfred A. Knopf, 1963.

Hudson-Weems, Clenora. *Africana Womanism: Reclaiming Ourselves.* Troy, MI: Bedford Publishers, Inc., 1993.

———. "Cultural and Agenda Conflicts in Academica: Critical Issues for Africana Women's Studies." *Western Journal of Black Studies* 13:4 (1989): 185–189.

———. "Self-naming and Self-Definition: An Agenda for Survival." *Sisterhood, Feminisms, and the Power.* Ed. Obioma Nnaemeka. Trenton, NJ: Africa World Press, 1998. 449–452.

Melhem, D.H. *Gwendolyn Brooks: Poetry and the Heroic Voice.* Lexington: KY: The University Press of Kentucky, 1987.

Monjo, Nicolas. "Young Girl Growing Up." *Saturday Review.* 36 (October 31, 1953): 36.

Morrison, Toni. *The Bluest Eye.* New York: The Penguin Group, 1970.

O'Daniel, Therman B., Introduction. *The Blacker the Berry . . . A novel of Negro Life.* 1929. New York: Macaulay Company, 1970.

Satz, Martha. "Honest Reporting: An Interview with Gwendolyn Brooks." *Southwest Review* 74: 1 (Winter 1989): 25–35.

Shaw, Harry B. "Maud Martha: The Way with Beauty." *In A Life Distilled: Gwendolyn Brooks, Her Poetry and Fiction.* Eds. Maria K. Mootry and Gary Smith. Urbana: University of Illinois Press, 1987. 254–270.

Thurman, Wallace. *The Blacker the Berry...A novel of Negro Life.* 1929. New York: Macaulay Company, 1970.

Washington, Mary Helen, ed. *Black-Eyed Susans.* New York: Anchor Books, 1975.

————."'The Darkened Eye Restored': Notes Toward a Literary History of Black Women." In *Reading Black, Reading Feminist.* Ed. Henry Louis Gates, Jr. New York: the Penguin Group, 1990. 30–42.

Contributors

Larry R. Andrews is currently Dean of Honors College and Associate Professor of English at Kent State University. He has also taught at the University of South Carolina, Warsaw University, and Volgograd State University. He has published articles and book chapters on Gwendolyn Brooks, Ann Petry, Gloria Naylor, and Russian and French fiction, as well as translations of Russian poetry and several pedagogical handbooks.

B. J. Bolden is Associate Professor of English at Chicago State University, Director of the Gwendolyn Brooks Center for Black Literature and Creative Writing, co-editor of *WarpLand: A Journal of Black Literature and Ideas,* and co-founder and Executive Vice President of the International Literary Hall of Fame for Writers of African Descent. She is co-chair of the Society for the Advancement of the Vivian G. Harsh Research Collection of Afro-American History and Literature, and chair of the Chicago Renaissance Project at the Carter G. Woodson Regional Library. She has published numerous scholarly articles including essays on Edgar Allan Poe, Diana Chang, Haki Madhubuti, Lucille Clifton, Sonia Sanchez, and Ntozake Shange. Her articles appear in *Historical Encyclopedia of Chicago Women, Reference Guide to American Literature, Black Women in America: An Historical Encyclopedia, and Contemporary Poets.* Her book of literary criticism is entitled *Urban Rage in Bronzeville: Social Commentary in the Poetry of Gwendolyn Brooks, 1945-1960* (Chicago: Third World Press, 1999).

Kelly Norman Ellis is Assistant Professor of English at Chicago State University. Her poetry appears in *Spirit and Flame, Sisterfire, Obsidian II, Calyx, Boomer Girls, Brightleaf*

Magazine, Fyah: An Online Literary Journal, the film "Coal Black Voices," and the upcoming CD collection, *She Laughs.* She is a founding member of the Affrilachian Poets, a traveling band of poets with roots in the South. Currently, she is completing a collection of poetry entitled "Tougaloo Blues." She lives with her partner, Kevin, and their baby daughter, Naomi Zora, in Chicago.

Regina Jennings is Assistant Professor of Africana Studies at Rutgers University. She is author of the following texts: *Midnight Morning Musings: Poems of an American African, Patriarchy, Resistance, and the Black Panther Party* forthcoming; "The Black Panther Party and the Poetics of Revolution" in progress. Some of her numerous scholarly articles appear in *The Journal of Black Studies, Pennsylvania English, Transformations, The Black Panther Party Reconsidered, Successful Women of Color and Their Daughters,* and *Africana History, Culture, and Social Policy.*

Dolores Kendrick was appointed Poet Laureate of the District of Columbia on May 14, 1999. She is the second person honored with the title, following Sterling Brown, who was appointed in 1984. She is the author of *Through the Ceiling, Now is the Thing to Praise,* and the award-winning book, *The Women of Plums: Poems in the Voices of Slave Women,* published in 1989. The theatrical performance adaptation of the book won the New York New Playwrights Award in 1997. Her rich history of poetic contributions to local and national publications has earned her numerous awards and honors, including a National Endowment for the Arts Award, and the prestigious Anisfield-Wolf Award. She was the first Vira I. Heinz Professor Emerita at Phillips Exeter Academy. Chicago State University has inducted her into the International Literary Hall of Fame for Writers of African Descent, an honor sponsored by the Gwendolyn Brooks Center for Black Literature and Creative Writing. Currently she is working on an adaptation of *The Women of Plums* for production at the National Theater, and she has been commissioned to write a poem that will be placed on a sculpture in front of the Martin Luther King Jr. Library in downtown Washington, DC.

D. H. Melhem is the author of five books of poetry, two critical works, one novel, a musical drama, a creative writing workbook, and over 50 published essays. Her *Gwendolyn Brooks: Poetry and the Heroic Voice* (University Press of Kentucky, 1987) was the first comprehensive study of the poet. It began as a doctoral dissertation at the CUNY Graduate Center where she received her degree and was nominated for a Woodrow Wilson Fellowship in Women's Studies. Her *Heroism in the New Black Poetry: Introductions and Interviews* was a National Endowment for the Humanities Fellowship Study and won an American Book Award. Winner of numerous awards for her poetry and her prose, she was most recently nominated for a CUNY Alumni Achievement Award and nominated a second time for a Pushcart Prize. With Leila Diab she is co-editor of *A Different Path: An Anthology of the Radius of Arab American Writers* (Ridgeway Press, 2000). She currently serves as vice-president of the International Women's Writing Guild.

Maria K. Mootry was the Director of African American Studies and Associate Professor of English at University of Illinois at Springfield. Her university teaching career included Northwestern University, Southern Illinois University at Carbondale, and Grinnell College. She was an internationally recognized scholar who co-edited the book, *A Life Distilled: Gwendolyn Brooks, Her Poetry and Fiction* (Urbana: University of Illinois Press, 1987). Her other scholarly works include plays, poetry, and research in bioethics. She was known also for her artistic and musical talent.

Adele S. Newson-Horst is full Professor and Chair of the Department of Africana Studies at the University of Michigan-Flint. As a Fulbright Professor, she served at an Afrikanna institution in South Africa in 1992. She was also a Fulbright-Hays participant in Africa in 1997. She wrote her dissertation on Zora Neale Hurston and later published it as *Zora Neale Hurston: A Reference Guide* (G. K. Hall). Some of her other scholarly publications include Black Communities in Transition: Voices from Southeast Florida (1996) co-edited with Abraham D. Lavender, and *Winds of Change: The Transforming Voices of Caribbean Women Writers and Scholars* (1998) co-edited with Linda Strong-Leek. She also contributes to *World Literature Today.*

Elaine Richardson is Assistant Professor of English at Pennsylvania State University. She has worked on a range of topics in applied linguistics, rhetoric and composition, language and literacy, and computers and literacy. Her current projects include a co-edited volume (with Ron Jackson) on "African American Rhetorics" (forthcoming), and a single authored monograph, "African American Centered Rhetoric and Composition."

Dorothy Randall Tsuruta is Associate Professor of Literature and Composition in Black Studies at San Francisco State University. She is editor of *The Black Studies Journal,* a publication of the Black Studies Department at San Francisco State University. She was a consultant and contributor to *Call and Response: The Riverside Anthology of The African Literary Tradition* (Houghton and Mifflin, 1998). Recent publications appear in *Concerns: A Publication of the Women's Caucus of the*

Modern Language Association (Spring 2000), and Sosongo *The Cameroon Review of the Arts* (June 2000). One of her essays will appear in *Contemporary Africana Theory and Thought* edited by Clenora Hudson Weems. Works in progress include "A Black Cannon: Rev. Elmer Augustus McLaughlin 1889-1994" and "Off Campus to Lunch: The Narrative of a Womanist on a Feminist Campus."

Editor

Jacqueline Bryant is an Associate Professor of English and Chairperson of the Department of English at Chicago State University. Her publications include articles in *Journal of Black Studies, WarpLand: A Journal of Black Literature and Ideas,* and *CLA Journal.* Her Book, The Foremother Figure in *Early Black Women's Literature: "Clothed in My Right Mind,"* is a part of the Studies in African American History and Culture Series, Garland Publishing (1999).

Secondary Readings on
Gwendolyn Brooks' *Maud Martha*

Bradley, Van Allen. Review. "Negro's Life Here Effectively
Portrayed in First Novel." *Chicago Daily News,*
30 September 1953, 26.

Butcher, Fanny. Review. "Swift, Sharp Prose by a Poet."
Chicago Sunday Tribune Magazine, 4 October 1953, 41.

Christian, Barbara. "Nuance and the Novella: A Study of
Gwendolyn Brooks's Maud Martha." *A Life Distilled:
Gwendolyn Brooks, Her Poetry and Fiction.* Eds. Maria K.
Mootry and Gary Smith. Urbana: University of Illinois
Press, 1987. 239–253.

Lattin, Patricia H. and Vernon E. Lattin. "Dual Vision in
Gwendolyn Brooks's *Maud Martha." On Gwendolyn
Brooks: Reliant Contemplation.* Ed. Stephen Caldwell
Wright. Ann Arbor: University of Michigan Press, 1996.
136–160.

Melhem, D. H. *Gwendolyn Brooks: Poetry and the Heroic Voice.*
Lexington: University Press of Kentucky, 1987. 90–95.

Monjo, Nicholas. Review. "Young Girl Growing Up."
Saturday Review, 30 October 1953, 41.

Park, You-me and Gayle Wald. "Native Daughters in the
Promised Land: Gender, Race, and the question of Separate
Spheres." *American Literature* 70.3 (1998): 607–633.

Rosenberger, Coleman. Review. "A Work of Art and Jeweled
Precision." *New York Herald Tribune Book Review,* 18
October 1953, 4.

Shands, Annette. "Gwendolyn Brooks as Novelist." *Black World* 22.8 (1973): 22–30.

Shaw, Harry B. "Maud Martha: The War with Beauty." *A Life Distilled: Gwendolyn Brooks, Her Poetry and Fiction.* Eds. Maria K. Mootry and Gary Smith. Urbana: University of Illinois Press, 1987. 254–270.

Walther, Malin LaVon. "Re-Wrighting Native: Gwendolyn Brooks's Domestic Aesthetic in Maud Martha." *Tulsa Studies in Women's Literature.* 13.1 (1994): 143–145.

Washington, Mary Helen. "'Taming All That Anger Down': Rage and Silence in Gwendolyn Brooks' Maud Martha." *Massachusetts Review.* 24 (1983): 453–466.

Washington, Mary Helen. "Plain, Black and Decently Wild: The Heroic Possibilities of Maud Martha." *The Voyage In: Fictions of Female Development.* Eds. Elizabeth Abel, Marianne Hirsch, and Elizabeth Langland. Hanover, NH: University Press of New England, 1983. 270–286.

Index

Notes

Notes

Notes

Notes

Notes

Notes

Notes

Notes